NEW
CAMBRIDGE PROFICIENCY

PRACTICE TESTS 2
for the Certificate of Proficiency in English

Nicholas Stephens
Rachel Finnie

NEW EDITIONS

Contents

Introduction 4

TEST ONE

Paper 1: **Reading**
An in-depth look 6
Exam technique 7
Hints on the multiple choice
lexical cloze (Part 1) 8
Test 9

Paper 2: **Writing**
An in-depth look 16
Exam technique 17
Test 18
Hints on writing for Part 1 19

Paper 3: **Use of English**
An in-depth look 20
Exam technique 20
Hints on how to gap-fill (Part 1) 21
Test 22

Paper 4: **Listening**
An in-depth look 28
Exam technique 28
Test 29

Paper 5: **Speaking**
An in-depth look 32
Exam technique 33
Test 34

TEST TWO

Paper 1: **Reading**
Hints on multiple choice (Part 2) 36
Test 37

Paper 2: **Writing**
Test 44
Hints on writing a report 45

Paper 3: **Use of English**
Hints on word formation (Part 2) 46
Test 47

Paper 4: **Listening**
Hints on sentence completion (Part 2) 52
Test 53

Paper 5: **Speaking**
Test 56
Most commonly-asked general questions 57

TEST THREE

Paper 1: **Reading**
Hints on the gapped text with
paragraphs removed (Part 3) 58
Test 59

Paper 2: **Writing**
Test 66
Hints on writing an article 67

Paper 3: **Use of English**
Hints on gap-filling sets of 3 sentences (Part 3) 68
Test 69

Paper 4: **Listening**
Hints on answering the multiple choice
sections (Parts 1 and 3) 74
Test 75

Paper 5: **Speaking**
Test 78
Hints on discussing pictures 79

TEST FOUR

Paper 1: **Reading**
Hints on one text with multiple choice
(Part 4) 80
Test 81

Paper 2: **Writing**
Test 88
Hints on writing a proposal 89

Paper 3: **Use of English**
Hints on sentence transformation (Part 4) 90
Test 91

Paper 4: **Listening**
Hints on how to decide
which speaker said what (Part 4) 96
Test 97

Paper 5: **Speaking**
Test 100
Hints on how to respond to
written questions (Part 3) 101

TEST FIVE

Paper 1: **Reading**
Hints on improving your chances 102
Test 103

Paper 2: **Writing**
Test 110
Hints on writing a review 111

Paper 3: **Use of English**
Hints on how to do Part 5 112
Test 113

Paper 4: **Listening**
Hints on completing the answer sheet 118
Test 119

Paper 5: **Speaking**
Test 122
Topics likely to appear 123

TEST SIX

Paper 1: **Reading**
Final tips for the exam 124
Test 125

Paper 2: **Writing**
Test 132
Hints on how to answer
the set book question 133
Final tips for the exam 133

Paper 3: **Use of English**
Final tips for the exam 134
Test 135

Paper 4: **Listening**
Final tips for the exam 140
Test 141

Paper 5: **Speaking**
Test 144
Final tips for the exam 145

TEST YOUR VOCABULARY

Test 1 146
Test 2 150
Test 3 154
Test 4 158
Test 5 162
Test 6 166

Photographs for the Speaking Papers 170

Introduction

What makes this Practice Test Book different from other test books available?

It is different because it is more than just a book of practice tests. It has been designed to not only familiarise students with the exact format of each part of the revised Cambridge Certificate of Proficiency in English (CPE), but also to expand their vocabulary and improve the skills required in the examination.

New Cambridge Proficiency Practice Tests 2 contains:

- six complete practice tests for the revised Cambridge Certificate of Proficiency in English
- full details about each paper
- exam technique sections – hints and tips for the student on how to approach each paper
- authentic reading passages
- extra *Test your vocabulary* exercises for the vocabulary used in each of the six tests
- listening practice containing a variety of accents, recorded by professional actors

The six tests in *New Cambridge Proficiency Practice Tests 2* can be completed by students at home as homework or in class as timed exercises. For maximum benefit it is recommended that teachers exploit the vocabulary content of the book by discussing the unknown vocabulary and getting the students to write it in their notebooks. Certain vocabulary could then be selected as the basis for discussion work, role-play or written work. The more students use the vocabulary for such activities, the more they will be able to use it naturally and incorporate it into their spoken and written work.

Cambridge Certificate of Proficiency in English (CPE): A brief outline of each paper

PAPER 1: READING (1 hour 30 minutes)

4 Parts:
- Part 1 – 3 short texts with 6 multiple choice cloze questions each. Students must choose which one of four words or phrases correctly completes the gap in the sentence.
- Part 2 – 4 short texts. After each text there are 2 four-option multiple choice questions.
- Part 3 – 1 text in which paragraphs have been removed. Students must decide from where in the text the paragraphs have been taken.
- Part 4 – 1 text with 7 four-option multiple choice questions.

All answers are written in pencil on a separate answer sheet.

PAPER 2: WRITING (2 hours)

Two compositions are to be written.

2 Parts:
- Part 1 – A compulsory question
- Part 2 – Students must answer one question from a choice of 4 questions (including the set book option).

Students answer in ink on lined paper provided by the invigilators.

Note: As the set books so frequently change, questions on them have not been included in this book. However, Test Five, Paper 2: Writing, contains hints and tips on how to answer set-book composition questions.

PAPER 3: USE OF ENGLISH (1 hour 30 minutes)

5 Parts:
- Part 1 – A short text with 15 gaps, each of which must be filled with one word.
- Part 2 – 10 word formation questions in one short text.
- Part 3 – 6 sets of 3 gapped sentences. Students must find the word that fits all 3 sentences in each question.
- Part 4 – 8 sentences that must be rewritten using a given word so that the meaning stays the same.
- Part 5 – 2 texts with 2 questions on each and a summary task.

Students answer in ink directly onto their question paper.

PAPER 4: LISTENING (approximately 40 minutes)

A cassette recording of 4 pieces, each of which is heard twice. Pieces include monologues, interviews, broadcasts, announcements, conversations, etc.

4 Parts: Part 1 – 4 extracts with 2 three-option multiple choice questions on each
           Part 2 – 9 sentence completion questions on one long text
           Part 3 – 5 four-option multiple choice questions on one long text
           Part 4 – 6 matching questions on one long text

Students answer directly onto their question paper and have five minutes at the end to transfer their answers in pencil onto a separate answer sheet.

PAPER 5: SPEAKING (19 minutes)

Students are interviewed in pairs.

3 Parts: Part 1 – Students are asked personal questions to help them relax.
           Part 2 – Students are shown photographs and asked questions about them. They have a discussion with each other using the photographs as prompts.
           Part 3 – Each student is given a written question to respond to individually. Then they have a discussion with each other, continuing the topics already discussed.

Grading System

Each of the five papers is worth 40 marks. The examination is worth 200 marks in total. In order to achieve a Grade C, candidates must achieve about 60% of the total marks.

Pass grades are A, B and C.

Fail grades are D and E.

On the day of the Proficiency examination

The written parts of the exam are normally taken on the first Sunday in December or the last Sunday in May and are in the following order:

Paper 2: Writing
Paper 1: Reading
Paper 3: Use of English
Paper 4: Listening

There are short breaks between each of the papers. Although you are given a time on your yellow form (*The Statement of Entry/Timetable*) from the British Council for the Listening paper, this time is often changed. Listen carefully when you take the Use of English paper as the invigilator will inform you then as to what time you will actually take the Listening paper.

The interview may be scheduled several days before or after the date of the written exam. Full details as to where and when will be stated on the yellow form.

You need to take the following with you to the examination centre:
- your yellow form (*The Statement of Entry/Timetable*)
- legal identification, such as a current passport or your ID card
- pencils
- blue or black pens
- a pencil sharpener
- an eraser

Test One — Paper 1: Reading

An in-depth look

You have one hour and a half to complete **Paper 1**: **Reading**. It tests your ability to understand written English.

The Reading paper has four parts.

PART 1
This is a four-option multiple choice lexical close. There are eighteen gaps to fill.

What is being tested?

- phrasal verbs
- idioms and expressions
- adverbial phrases
- words appropriate to the context
- collocations
- word groups

You need a wide range of vocabulary to succeed in this part of the examination. To achieve this, you must learn to record and learn new vocabulary systematically. Try learning whole phrases rather than words in isolation. Reading books and articles in English outside the classroom will also help you immeasurably.

PART 2
This consists of four short texts from a range of sources. After each text there are two four-option multiple choice questions. The four texts have between 600-900 words in total.

To answer the questions which follow each passage, read the text carefully. Understanding every single word is not necessary. To help yourself cope with the unknown vocabulary you will probably encounter in the exam, you need to practise deducing the meaning of unknown words from the context.

You will be tested on your understanding of different aspects of the passage, such as its main point or points, the writer's opinion or attitude, the theme or gist of the text and the overall purpose of the passage.

PART 3
There is one text from a variety of possible sources. It is between 800-1100 words. Paragraphs have been removed from the text and placed in a jumbled order after it. You have to decide from where in the text the paragraphs have been taken. There is one extra paragraph which does not fit in the text.

Here you are being tested on how you understand a text. That is, how a text is structured, what cohesive devices are employed and general understanding.

You will need to practise being able to follow the order of a text from the beginning to the end. Being able to spot linking devices will help you. One idea is to cut up magazine stories and then piece them back together.

PART 4
This is one text from a variety of possible sources. It is between 700-850 words in length. It has seven four-option multiple choice questions.

Like Part 2 you are tested on being able to understand the purpose of a text, its gist, what the writer's opinion is, etc. Once again, any extra reading you do will help.

Grading system and answer sheet
Each correct answer in Part 1 is worth one mark.
Each correct answer in Part 2, Part 3 and Part 4 is worth two marks.
You need to correctly answer at least 60% (ie, 24 marks out of 40) to guarantee passing this paper.

You will mark your answers in pencil on a separate answer sheet, which will be scanned by computer. The test must be completed within the hour and a half allotted; extra time is not given to transfer your answers to the answer sheet.

Test One

Exam technique

Knowing how to approach the **Reading** part of the examination is as important as knowing the grammar and vocabulary.

You have only one hour and thirty minutes, so timing and pacing yourself is crucial. You should spend no more than twenty minutes on each part. Timing is something that you can start practising now as you work through this book, whether you do the practice tests at school, in a private lesson or at home.

Wear a watch to the examination centre and pace yourself throughout.

Answer every question. This is, after all, a multiple-choice exam and even by guessing, you stand at least a 25% chance of being correct.

Keeping calm, being familiar with the answer sheet, pacing yourself carefully and having a pencil, pencil sharpener and eraser with you will help you feel more relaxed and confident in your approach to this paper.

Never rush through a paper. A specific amount of time is allocated for each paper for a reason – that is how long it should take you to complete that particular paper. If you finish early, use the time to check your work. It could mean the difference between passing or failing.

Test One

Paper 1: Reading

Hints on the multiple choice lexical cloze (Part 1)

This is a four-option multiple choice lexical close. There are three texts and eighteen gaps to fill.

The missing word or words can be part of an idiom (eg, *pull someone's leg*), a phrasal verb (eg, *branch out*), a set phrase (eg, *at your earliest convenience*), or a collocation (e.g. *bitterly disappointed*). They might also depend on semantic precision, ie, choosing the most appropriate word for a particular context.

When you are given a choice of synonyms, often the correct answer does not depend only on meaning and general context, but also the kinds of words that come directly before or after the missing words. A common example of this is when only one of the synonyms is followed by the particular preposition that comes after the gap.

You need a wide range of vocabulary to succeed in this part of the examination. To achieve this, reading books and articles in English outside the classroom will help you. You must also learn to record and learn new vocabulary systematically. Try learning whole phrases rather than words in isolation.

Test One

Part 1

For questions **1-18**, read the three texts below and decide which answer (**A**, **B**, **C**, or **D**) best fits each gap.

BOOKS BY 'CELEBRITIES'

The past decade or so has seen an increasing number of famous people (1) .... their celebrity status by getting their autobiographies published. Those eager to jump on the (2) .... have included politicians, footballers, models and TV personalities. Normally their life stories have been written in a style (3) .... the successful tabloid formula – sensational and scandalous. Indeed, such is the thirst for high-class gossip that the list of writers exploiting this demand has (4) .... beyond the rich and famous. Now, it seems, anyone (5) .... connected with a celebrity who has a tale to tell can reap financial rewards in this manner.

So, if ever I am strapped for cash in the future, my (6) .... encounter with the Prime Minister may qualify me to write at least a feature article in a well-known tabloid.

1	A	cashing in on	B	brushing up on	C	getting up to	D	squaring up to
2	A	applecart	B	bandwagon	C	roundabout	D	roller-coaster
3	A	in line with	B	in terms of	C	by means of	D	in keeping with
4	A	surpassed	B	broadened	C	extended	D	expanded
5	A	barely	B	remotely	C	virtually	D	roughly
6	A	ephemeral	B	small	C	short	D	brief

A REAL CHALLENGE

Having a reputation as someone who never shies away from a challenge, I readily accepted an invitation to go scuba diving with a group of friends. Although it had been quite some time since my previous underwater experience, I felt that I was capable of (7) .... my own with this team of divers. After all, once you have learnt a skill, it is (8) .... a matter of time before it all (9) .... back to you.

So there I was, waiting confidently at the roadside for my friends to pick me up when a blue van (10) .... alongside. As the door slid open, I climbed in only to see state-of-the-art diving equipment that made mine appear (11) .... ancient. It was at this point that I realised I was about to be tested to the (12) .... extent of my abilities.

7	A	having	B	holding	C	getting	D	taking
8	A	almost	B	hardly	C	easily	D	simply
9	A	comes	B	goes	C	returns	D	arrives
10	A	came up	B	turned up	C	got in	D	pulled up
11	A	extremely	B	positively	C	very	D	exceptionally
12	A	complete	B	total	C	full	D	whole

GEORGE

George had become decidedly moodier since he got (13) .... of the rumour that he was the (14) .... candidate for a transfer to the company's Madrid office. He'd spend long, uninterrupted periods brooding in his office – behaviour more commonly associated with someone suffering from clinical depression. George's colleagues, though obviously sympathetic towards his plight, would not support him, preferring instead to (15) .... themselves from the feud simmering between him and their Texan manager, Greg Dawson. They were fully aware that George should not have been (16) .... for promotion in favour of Dawson, but they remained silent for (17) .... of falling out of favour. They didn't want to be next in line for a transfer or worse. George, however, was determined to put up a (18) .... .

13	A	news	B	wind	C	information	D	facts
14	A	prime	B	lead	C	top	D	major
15	A	remove	B	distance	C	extricate	D	separate
16	A	taken out	B	gone through	C	left out	D	passed over
17	A	hazard	B	danger	C	fear	D	risk
18	A	fight	B	stand	C	conflict	D	battle

Paper 1: Reading

Part 2

You are going to read four extracts which are all concerned in some way with money. For questions 19-26, choose the answer (**A, B, C** or **D**) which you think fits best according to the text.

NOTICE OF CHANGES TO THE FORMAT OF A BANK STATEMENT
Your revised statement format will contain the following features:

- The dates of the interest charging period will be slightly different to those of account charges. This change will have no effect on the overall amounts you will pay, or when these amounts are debited. Both of these periods will be detailed on your pre-advice.

- Any credit interest will now appear on the first working day after the period in which it is calculated, rather than the last working day of the month.

- The credit interest entry on your statement will no longer show the tax that is deducted from it. The next statements we send you will no longer contain a summary of the interest received or tax paid in the previous tax year. Instead, you will receive a separate formal certificate of interest for the previous tax year.

- Most regular charges to your account will be added together and appear as a single, total amount on your statement. These changes will be detailed on your pre-advice.

- If you use your debit card abroad, your statement will now include the date and time of the transaction and the last four digits of your card number. The exchange rate will not be shown. However, we will be happy to inform you of this if you ask at any branch.

---

19 Where will the amount of tax now appear?
   A on a form issued on the last working day of each month
   B on the new style of bank statement
   C on a certificate issued by the tax office
   D on a special certificate stating interest for the previous tax year

20 Details of exchange rates on transactions abroad will be
   A included on the pre-advice.
   B shown next to the date of the transaction.
   C given on request.
   D provided on presentation of part of the card number.

Poverty in the 1800s

Filthy both inside and outside, the houses in the slums are occupied from the cellar to the attic. Their appearance is such that no human being could possibly wish to live in them. But all this is nothing compared with the dwellings in the narrow alleys between the streets, entered by covered passages between the houses, in which the filth and tottering ruin surpass all description. Scarcely a whole windowpane can be found here. The walls are crumbling, door posts and window frames are loose and broken. Doors are made of old boards nailed together, or are altogether wanting in the thieves' quarter, where no doors are needed since there is nothing to steal. Heaps of garbage and ashes lie everywhere, and the foul liquids emptied outside the doors gather in stinking pools. Here the poorest of the poor, the worst-paid workers with thieves and the victims of circumstance indiscriminately huddle together. They are set to drown in the whirlpool of ruin which surrounds them, sinking deeper day by day and losing their power to resist the demoralising influence of want, filth and their evil surroundings.

---

21 What does the writer imply about the people living in the area described?
   A They have good community spirit.
   B Their futures are uncertain.
   C They are doomed.
   D They have good survival instincts.

22 What is the main characteristic of the area?
   A the dirt
   B the crime rate
   C the cold
   D immorality

Test One

BLACK MARK FOR ELITE CREDIT CARD

A renowned bank has been forced to defend the reputation of its most prestigious credit card after a series of blunders led a client to cancel his membership.

The charge card is issued by invitation only to some of the bank's wealthiest customers. It promises some lavish perks. For example, its concierge service claims to be able to organise holidays, arrange theatre tickets or book a restaurant anywhere in the world at a moment's notice. But the experience of Greg Quine suggests the service falls short of expectations.

He said, 'I believed the membership fee of £650 would provide me with a service that made my life easier, but it has let me down more than once. I became so frustrated that I cancelled my card.'

When Quine asked for a weekend break to be arranged, one of the hotels could not arrange a cot for his 18-month-old daughter.

There were also mishaps when he went to pick up a hire car and when he asked for a specific gift to be bought from Tiffany & Co.

When Quine complained to the bank in writing, it took the firm almost three weeks to respond. He then tried to contact a senior member of the company's travel department by phone, but his call was not returned.

Although the company said it understood Quine's frustration, it added, 'In our experience, it is very rare for a customer to be unhappy with the service.'

23 Why did Mr Quine cancel his credit card?
   A He believed that the membership fee was too high.
   B He was disappointed by the extra services promised.
   C It was far too difficult to use.
   D The hotel he was booked into was of a low standard.

24 Which word best sums up the bank's reaction to the complaints?
   A dismissive
   B disappointed
   C apologetic
   D rude

BARTER

In the days before the use of coins, how much would it have cost to purchase a pig? Two sheep? A barrel of ale? Twenty hens? How is it possible to establish a value for the pig from a comparison of such wildly differing commodities? The answer lies ultimately in what the pig's owner and the pig's purchaser consider to be a fair offer of exchange and their respective abilities to haggle.

Barter is a system of exchange that is terribly inefficient and highly inflexible. Our pig farmer, for instance, must first find someone who wants the pig and can offer something desirable in exchange. Once such an individual has been found, it is still uncertain whether a mutually agreeable value can be found for the exchange of the pig. For these reasons, many economic historians argue that even the simplest of traditional societies used some form of money. Money removes the constraints of barter. The pig farmer could set a price for the pig and, having sold it to a willing buyer, he could then set about purchasing other things even though the sellers of those other products might have no desire whatsoever for a pig. Given the obvious advantages and convenience that money affords, it is clear that if barter occurs today, it does so out of necessity rather than choice. So, when barter does appear in an economy, we know the market is failing to function as it should.

25 The successful use of barter depends mostly on
   A supply and demand.
   B compromise.
   C cost analysis.
   D price fixing.

26 According to the text,
   A the use of barter is limited.
   B a free market economy is a relatively new concept.
   C societies cannot exist without money.
   D farmers were good at haggling.

Paper 1: Reading

Part 3

You are going to read an extract from a travel writer's account of a visit to Churchill, Manitoba, in Canada. Seven paragraphs have been removed from the extract. Choose from the paragraphs **A–H** the one which best fits each gap (**27–33**). There is one extra paragraph which you do not need to use.

The distance from the helicopter to the lodge looks a good twenty-second dash, hindered as I am by heavy camera equipment and a bone-numbing lethargy caused by a biting wind chilling the temperature to -20°C.

27

For this particular town describes itself as the polar bear capital of the world and without the bears, it would struggle to exist. The town is a testament to the fact that eco-tourism is big business, a force for regeneration. In October, Canada's bears start their migration north into the Arctic, where they devour seals with abandon and nearly double their body weight. Situated on the south-western edge of the mighty Hudson Bay, the settlement lies slap bang in the path of the bears as they head for colder climes.

28

This is vaguely reassuring and extremely thrilling. As I peg it across the frozen tundra that borders Hudson Bay, I sense my guide's gun trained on the middle distance, ready to pick off a bear in a flash. Another guide armed with a shotgun rushes out to meet me. Bravely, I dart past him into the warm confines of what was once a saloon.

29

Today it is a wildlife lodge, protected by sturdy bars which form an encapsulating cage, keeping the humans in and the bears out like a sort of inverse zoo. There is something surreal about eating piping-hot spaghetti bolognese while a frustrated man-eater eyes you hungrily from less than one metre away.

30

You cannot reach the town by car. Most people who make the journey prefer to avoid the slow train and come in by plane from Winnipeg in the south of Manitoba, a three-hour trip. Winnipeg itself is almost three hours by plane from Toronto. Churchill is not a place you stumble across. Many of the town's inhabitants have travelled no more than fifty miles away in their lives.

31

There is also the Aurora Borealis, or Northern Lights as it is more prosaically known. This natural phenomenon is particularly popular among Japanese honeymooners who believe that the Aurora will make their offspring grow up to be healthy, wealthy and wise.

32

But it is the bears that really draw the crowds. As the bay freezes and the water coagulates, huge slabs of ice float up into the Arctic Circle. The bears roam the ice, hunting seals. Sometimes they wait by air holes, waiting to drag an unfortunate seal out of the sea by its neck. Sometimes the bear will catch the seal napping, though this is less usual. Either way, on average a typical polar bear eats a seal every five or six days during winter.

33

The weather is variable and governs how many bears you are likely to see. When I went (the first week of November), the ice had had plenty of time to form and most of the dominant males had departed in search of seals. The mother seals and their young were still waiting to venture onto the ice to avoid male bears, which eat their cubs, and were hunting somewhere south of Churchill.

A Actually, it's no longer an alcoholics' paradise and purveyor of dubious moral entertainment. The White Whale lodge, one of Churchill's oldest buildings, was a house of ill repute until the Thirties. For decades it served the navvies who worked on the railway and in the port in this small, inhospitable town (population 1000 in a good month), which made most of its money by exporting wheat to Europe.

B The extreme temperatures make it difficult to stay outside the buggies for more than five minutes, no matter how many layers of clothing you are wearing. If you think that ski-wear will suffice, forget it: you'll perish. The tour operator can arrange for you to rent the sort of clothing that would not look out of place on a moon landing.

C Before the feast, the bears roam the edge of the bay waiting for the ice to form. This is when Churchill becomes a mecca for eco-tourists. Depending on how quickly the cold bites, the bear-watching season runs for between five and seven weeks, roughly from the beginning of October to mid-November.

D It's a fair bet that if there are polar bears nearby, they will pounce and rip me to shreds in seconds. This would do a great deal to put Churchill, one of Canada's truly remote towns, on the global map, though not for the reasons its inhabitants would like.

E So thank heavens for the bears, without which Churchill would almost certainly cease to exist. Actually, it's more than just the bears that pull in the punters. In the summer, when the temperature has been known to reach 22°C, Churchill is home to hundreds of Beluga whales and numerous species of bird life. Fishing is said to be good, too, attracting anglers from far and wide.

F The huge mammals can move at speeds of 50 kilometres per hour, even those that weigh more than 450 kilos and stand over 3 metres tall on their back legs. They look sleepy, the result of not having eaten for months, but the merest whiff of food will send them charging across the ice. The pilot told me shortly before we took off for the lodge, 'Run straight from the 'copter to the lodge. I have a gun.'

G No one is quite sure where this myth originated, although someone has suggested that its roots date back to the success achieved by the child of a couple from the land of the rising sun who had visited the area as newlyweds.

H These days the railway still runs – three times a week – but the port is not so busy. The massive shipments of wheat are not so regular and there is speculation that one day the port may close altogether. The huge US Army base disappeared in the 1980s, leaving Canada's second-longest runway and a motley collection of prefabs as a legacy.

Paper 1: Reading

Part 4

You are going to read an extract from a book about human behaviour. For questions **34-40**, choose the answer (**A**, **B**, **C**, or **D**) which you think fits best according to the text.

ACTIONS

All animals perform actions and most do little else. A great many also make artifacts – constructed or manufactured objects – such as nests, webs, beds and burrows. Among the monkeys and apes there is also some evidence of abstract thinking. But it is only with humans that artifaction and abstraction have run riot. This is the essence of the success of humankind. With their massive brains, humans have increasingly internalised their behaviour through complex processes of abstract thought – through language, philosophy and mathematics. With their weak bodies, they have dramatically externalised their behaviour, scattering the surface of the globe with their artifacts – their machines, weapons, vehicles, roads, works of art, buildings, villages and cities.

There they sit, these thinking, building animals, their machines humming gently all around and their thoughts whirring inside their heads. Artifaction and abstraction have come to dominate their lives. One might almost suppose that action – simple animal action – would be beneath them, surviving only as a remnant from their primeval past. But this is not so. Throughout it all, they have remained creatures of action – gesticulating, posturing, moving, expressive primates. They are as far today from becoming the disembodied, giant superbrains of science fiction as they were back in their prehistoric hunting past. Philosophy and engineering have not replaced animal activity. They have added to it. The fact that we have developed a concept of happiness and given words to express it does not stop us from performing the action pattern of stretching our lips into a smile. Nor does the fact that we have boats prevent us from swimming.

Our hunger for action is as strong as it has ever been. City dwellers, however, deeply impressed they may be by the achievements of abstraction and artifaction, still take their pleasure in age-old fashion. They eat, drink and go to parties where they can laugh, frown, gesture and embrace. When they take their holidays, their machines bear them away to a few snatched weeks in forests, on hills and seashores, where they can re-live their animal past in the pursuit of simple physical activities such as walking, climbing and swimming.

From an objective standpoint, there is a curious irony about a human animal flying a thousand miles in a machine costing several million pounds in order to splash about in a rock pool, looking for seashells. Or another who has spent all day operating a powerful computer and then goes home and puts on an apron to be the cook at a barbecue held in his back garden. Yet this is what people do, tacitly accepting the irresistible need to express themselves in simple bodily actions.

What form do these actions take, and how are they acquired by each individual? Human behaviour is not free-flowing; it is divided up into a long series of separate events. Each event, such as eating a meal, visiting a theatre, or taking a bath has its own special rules and rhythms. During our lifetimes, we can expect to experience a total of over a million such behaviour events. Each of these events is itself subdivided into numerous distinct acts. Basically, these acts follow one another in a sequence of posture-movement-posture-movement. Most of the postures we adopt and the movements we make have been performed thousands of times before. Most of them are performed unconsciously, spontaneously and without self-analysis. In many cases, they are so familiar that we do not even know how we do them. For example, when people interlock their fingers, one thumb rests on top of the other. For each person there's a dominant thumb in this action and whenever left and right hand interlock, the same thumb rests uppermost. Yet few people can guess which is their dominant thumb without going through the motions of interlocking their hands and looking to see which thumb comes out on top. Over the years, each person has developed a fixed pattern of interlocking without realising it. If they try to reverse the positions, bring the dominant thumb beneath the other, the hand posture will feel strange and awkward.

This is only a trivial example, but almost every body action performed by adults has a characteristic fixed pattern. These Fixed Action Patterns are the basic units of behaviour that the human field-observer employs as his points of reference. He watches their form, the context in which they occur and the messages they transmit. He also asks questions about how they were acquired in the first place. Were they inborn, requiring no prior experience whatsoever? Were they discovered by personal trial and error as each person grew older? Were they absorbed as people unconsciously emulated their companions? Or were they acquired by conscious training, being learned by deliberate effort based on specific analytical observation, or active teaching?

34 Humans are unique in that they
   A are capable of abstract thought.
   B are highly active.
   C have been so creative.
   D are able to build structures.

35 Which of the following has been responsible for the degree of human artifaction?
   A subconscious stimuli
   B the ability to wage war
   C their domination of other species
   D advanced thought processes

36 How does the writer appear to view humans in the opening paragraph?
   A as intrinsically powerless animals
   B as impressive
   C as a species to be feared
   D as having highly destructive natures

37 According to the writer, modern humans
   A have reached the end of their evolutionary road.
   B only need to express concepts through language.
   C are reminiscent of fictitious characters.
   D have extended their basic behaviour through technology.

38 The writer considers humans' need to engage in simple activities as
   A strangely ironic.
   B old-fashioned.
   C fascinating to anthropologists.
   D an outlet for excess energy.

39 How are behaviour events described?
   A They are performed self-consciously.
   B They can be broken down into their constituent parts.
   C They require careful consideration.
   D They are unique to each individual.

40 How do observers of human behaviour operate?
   A They initially treat behaviour as being instinctive.
   B They analyse behaviour methodically.
   C They first determine how common a particular type of behaviour is.
   D They each have their own ways of conducting research.

Test One — Paper 2: Writing

An in-depth look

You have two hours to complete **Paper 2: Writing**. You are required to write two compositions of 300-350 words each. Part 1 is a compulsory task and in Part 2 you have a choice of four subjects. There are five different task types.

In **Part 1**, you will be asked to write one of the following:

- article
- essay
- letter
- proposal

In **Part 2**, you will be asked to choose from 4 of the following:

- article
- essay
- letter
- proposal
- review
- report

Part 1 requires you to produce discursive writing, which means that you will have to present an argument and develop it, express an opinion and support it with evidence.

Part 2 requires you to describe, evaluate, summarise or relay information from a rubric or make recommendations in a persuasive manner. An important difference between the two parts is that in the second you must refer more directly to the details presented to you in the question or invent such details yourself, and rely less on your own opinions. In other words, while in Part 1 you are using the details in the question as a starting point, in Part 2 you must put yourself more in the specific context which has been presented to you in the question.

Each of the five tasks requires a different style of writing and choice of vocabulary. Use a range of structures, tenses and vocabulary to answer the task and make sure you stay on topic. One of the things the examiners will be assessing is your ability to organise your writing.

You answer on lined paper provided by the examination centre. You must write in **blue** or **black pen**.

Test One

Exam technique

You have **two** hours to write **two compositions**. This is ample time for this paper, but you still need to be aware of the time. It is pointless spending one and a half hours on the first essay and trying to write the second in thirty minutes.

- Do not waste time writing out the question. Just put the question number.

- Plan or make notes on what points you want to include and organise them into paragraphs. Make sure your plan answers the question. Not answering the question or staying on topic is the reason why most students fail this paper. If this is the case, you need to make adjustments to your work.

- Write your essay while keeping an eye on the time.

- Do an approximate word count by choosing a line which appears to have an average number of words and count them. Multiply this number by the number of lines you have written. If the essay is longer than the correct length, the marker draws a line at the approximate place where the correct length is reached. Although what is written after this point is still taken into account, closer inspection is given to what comes before the line. You may lose marks.

  Conversely, if your work is too short, you will also lose marks.

  Remember, every word is a word. **A**, **an** and **the** are all words and must be included when you count how much you have written.

- Read your essay through and correct any grammar, spelling or vocabulary errors and then leave it until you finish the second composition.

- Look at all four options in Part 2 and decide which you can answer the best. Think about your choices carefully. If the rubric asks for an article, then it must look and be written like an article. The same holds true for a report. Can you do either of these well? Are you confident about writing an article? Think about the type of vocabulary you will have to use, the grammar (particularly tenses) and the topic. Do you know anything about it? And last but not least, do you understand every word in the question? Do not guess what the question means. If you are not sure you understand it completely, **do not attempt it**.

- When you have finished your second composition, go back to the first one and read it again. You are more likely to see mistakes when you have had a break from it. Then check your second essay again.

Most students do not take the full two hours to complete this paper but you should not rush through it.
Take your time and check what you have written carefully.

Remember to take two or three pens with you.

Test One

Paper 2: Writing

Part 1

You must answer this question. Write your answer in **300-350** words in an appropriate style.

1   You have read the extract below as part of a newspaper article on the gradual disappearance of the traditional family. Readers were asked to send in their opinions. You decide to write a **letter** responding to the points raised and expressing your own views.

> The significance of the family within society has diminished due to women pursuing professional careers and neglecting their duties as mothers. And what makes matters worse is that they wish to be treated as equals and yet exploit their femininity in order to manipulate men at the same time. I say it is time to restore the traditional family to its rightful status as the cornerstone of our society. Is there anybody out there who shares my views?

Write your **letter**. Do not write any postal addresses.

Part 2

Write an answer to one of the questions **2-4** in this part. Write your answer in **300-350** words in an appropriate style.

2   You are a researcher employed by your local council. You have been asked to write a proposal on how the area on which an old school stands could be best used after the buildings have been pulled down. Within your proposal you should include ideas on what facilities are currently needed and how the town would benefit from your proposals.

Write your **proposal**.

3   You have recently attended an annual exhibition called *Technology in Progress*. Write a review for a local newspaper commenting on all aspects of the event.

Write your **review**.

4   Your local newspaper has invited readers to contribute an article about changes that have taken place in your neighbourhood in recent years. You have decided to send in an article.

Write your **article**.

Test One

Hints on writing for Part 1

Whatever writing format is given in Part 1, you will be expected to produce a discursive piece of writing. Discursive writing should include:

- a **good introduction** and not just a reiteration of the question.
- a **balanced argument** – there are always two sides to any discussion.
- an **impersonal point of view**. Try not to use 'I' but variations of 'It is believed/said/thought...' or 'Some people say/think...', etc.
- a **conclusion** that summarises in two or three sentences your main arguments. Do not introduce new points in your conclusion.
- good use of **connectors**.

Always plan your compositions before writing them. The following is an example of a plan:

Paragraph 1	Introduce the subject in general terms. You can suggest which side you are on but do not reach a conclusion yet.
Paragraph 2	Think of some arguments for the other side.
Paragraph 3	State why you disagree with these arguments and state your own opinion.
Paragraph 4	Conclude by summarising your personal opinion in two or three sentences.

Tips

If you write a composition where you are strongly in favour of something or against it, remember that others may have different opinions. It is more effective to mention them and then show they are wrong than not to mention them at all.

Some of the discursive topics in recent years have included:

- Do you agree that advertising encourages people to spend money?
- Discuss the harmful or beneficial effects on society of the media.
- Discuss whether teaching children a language should include more than just the language.
- Do you agree that the private lives of public people should be made public?
- Discuss whether in modern life people have time for themselves.
- Do you think too much money is spent on health care?
- Discuss the effects of modern technology on everyday life.
- Does having satellite television help us to understand people from other cultures better?

Test One — Paper 3: Use of English

An in-depth look

You have one hour and thirty minutes to complete **Paper 3: Use of English** which is in five parts.

Part 1
This is an open cloze which comprises fifteen gaps. The cloze is to be completed with one word in each gap. Correct spelling is essential. One mark is awarded for each correct answer.

Part 2
This is a word formation exercise. You have to complete a text containing ten gaps. Each gap corresponds to a word. The 'stems' of the missing words are next to the text and have to be transformed to provide the missing words. One mark is given for each correct answer.

Part 3
This consists of six questions. Each question is made up of three separate sentences which contain a gap. You have to find one word which can be used to complete all three sentences. You are being tested on such things as collocation, phrasal verbs, idioms and the patterns in which lexical items occur. Two marks are given for each correct answer.

Part 4
Here there are eight questions comprising a gapped sentence which must be completed using a word given, so that it has a similar meaning to the lead-in sentence. Two marks are given for each correct answer.

Part 5
Here you are given two texts with two questions on each text. Two marks are given for each question. You also have to write a summary using relevant information from both texts. Fourteen marks are given for the summary; four marks are awarded for content and ten marks for writing skills. Your summary should be between 50-70 words and very short or long ones will be marked down. You need to be very careful with spelling and punctuation. You will not be penalised for using American spelling, but you must be consistent. You will be penalised if you use both British and American spelling.

Grading system
The total number of marks for the Use of English paper is 75, which is scaled down to 40. You need to obtain roughly 60% to pass this paper, which is a score of 24.

Exam technique

You have **one hour and thirty minutes** to complete the Use of English paper. It is probably a good idea to work through Parts 1, 2, 3 and 4 as quickly as possible so you do not feel pressed for time when you come to write your summary. Should you prefer to do Part 5 first, try not to spend more than half an hour on it so you have ample time for the rest of the paper. Do not leave any questions unanswered. Always make a guess when you don't know the answer.

You will be tested on both your grammatical and lexical abilities. Learning words, idioms and expressions in context will benefit you when you approach this paper.

Always try to write your answers clearly and neatly. A candidate can fail the exam if the examiner cannot read their writing.

Each of the five questions in this paper will be looked at in more detail throughout this book.

> **Note**: For Parts 1-3, you must write on the answer sheet in CAPITAL LETTERS with a soft pencil. You do not have to write in capital letters for Parts 4 and 5.

Test One

Hints on how to gap-fill (Part 1)

First of all, it is important to read the text all the way through so that you know what the passage is about and start to get an idea of what type of words are missing.

Then go back through the text, filling in the most obvious words that you know from your first reading. You are left with gaps that, as yet, you do not know the answer to. Look at the words surrounding each gap, especially those in the same sentence, to find anything which can help you decide the meaning and grammatical form of the missing word.

For example:

> *Ironically, the harder he worked, the .... tired he felt.*

The gap is testing your knowledge of parallel structures with comparatives that show how different things change together. The word *Ironically* at the beginning indicates that the sentence is describing something contrary to what is expected. As a result, the answer is not *more* but *less*.

When you have completed the text, look very carefully at each word that you have written and ask yourself:

- Does it have a logical meaning in its sentence and in the passage as a whole?
- Is it grammatically correct?

Then read the passage all the way through to check that the words you have put in make sense, not just in each sentence but also in each paragraph and in the context of the whole text. Sometimes a word that looks correct in a sentence can be incorrect when you consider the meaning of the whole paragraph.

If you really cannot think of a word and have looked at all the clues in the sentence, leave the gap-filling, finish the next exercise and come back to the gap-filling. Sometimes having a break from it helps you to find the word when you return to the exercise.

You are being tested on your awareness of grammatical structure and lexico-grammatical structure. Consequently, words surrounding a gap may give you clues as to what the missing word is. Look for prepositions before and after the gap and think about collocations with prepositions, such as *operate on*, *rely on*, etc. Relative pronouns, modal verbs, the definite and indefinite article, prepositions, auxiliary verbs, etc, are all tested.

Some of the most difficult kinds of words which you need to fill gaps with in this part are determiners. These may be articles (eg, *a, an, the*), possessive pronouns (eg, *my, hers, their, its*), pronouns and adjectives beginning with wh (eg, *which, what, whatever, whichever*), demonstrative pronouns (eg, *this, that, these, those*), and quantifiers (eg, *some, any, no, each, every, more, less*).

Remember to fill every gap. Only give **one**-word answers and read the entire passage when you have finished. Make sure that your spelling is correct.

Learning words and expressions in context, especially grammatical patterns and collocations, will help you in this part of the exam.

> **Note**: For Parts 1-3 of the Use of English paper, you must write on the answer sheet in CAPITAL LETTERS with a soft pencil. You do not have to write in capital letters for Parts 4 and 5.

Test One

Paper 3: Use of English

Part 1

For questions **1-15**, read the text below and think of the word which best fits each space. Use only one word in each space. There is an example at the beginning (**0**).

Example: | **0** | OVER |

Killer smog

A dense fog settled (0) ......OVER...... London (1) .... the night of 4 December 1952. Held in place by cold air above and no wind to (2) .... it away, the fog grew thicker, trapping in (3) .... clutches the smoke of a million open coal fires. The streets were (4) .... of a choking, sulphurous smog. (5) .... were hospital wards. Many people went to bed feeling tired and never woke up. In some parts of the East End, the death rates were seven (6) .... their normal level.

When the smog lifted, ministers had some questions to answer. Why had this smog been so lethal? What could be done to prevent (7) .... one from descending on the city? And most pressing of (8) .... , how could the public be persuaded the government had a grip (9) .... the situation?

Seeing no alternative (10) .... burning coal, the ministers decided that doctors should prescribe up to two million cheap masks to people (11) .... from heart and respiratory diseases. (12) .... they knew the masks would offer (13) .... if any protection against smog, they (14) .... ahead with the plan, a decision that would (15) .... many more Londoners their lives over the coming months.

Part 2

For questions **16-25**, read the text below. Use the word given in capitals at the end of some of the lines to form a word that fits in the space in the same line. There is an example at the beginning (**0**).

Example: | 0 | PROPOSITION |

Four Colours Suffice – a book review

In 1852, a mathematician put forward a (0) ...PROPOSITION... which   PROPOSE
was the height of (16) .... Francis Guthrie noticed   SIMPLE
that on a map of England you only need four colours to
(17) .... that no two adjacent counties are the same   SURE
hue. He also suggested that this was true for any map on a
plane surface. However, proof of his simple theory turned out
to be highly (18) .... and the problem captured the   ELUDE
imaginations of many amateurs and professionals over the
following century. Finally, in 1976 an (19) .... of three   ALLY
mathematicians produced proof of the theory in a report
which was hundreds of pages long.

At first glance, the facts may seem (20) .... , but in   INSPIRE
his new book, (21) .... Four Colours Suffice, Robin Wilson   TITLE
provides a fascinating (22) .... into how mathematics moves   SEE
forward, how approaches have changed over the past century and
a half, and how (23) .... dedicated and often eccentric   NUMBER
mathematicians (24) .... pursued the proof of Guthrie's   RELENT
theorem.

His conclusion, not unlike that of other writers, is that no matter
how (25) .... computers become, there will always be a   DISPENSE
place for human experts to provide the colour so desperately needed
in potentially dry subjects like mathematics.

Paper 3: Use of English

Part 3

For questions **26-31**, think of one word only which can be used appropriately in all three sentences. Here is an example (**0**).

Example:

0   After being responsible for two .... starts, the athlete was disqualified from the sprint.
    I couldn't understand what Grandma was saying until she put in her .... teeth.
    Making a .... statement to the police is an offence.

    | 0 | FALSE |

26 After having to walk up six flights of stairs, the elderly couple were desperately .... of breath.
    Marcie's attempt to look younger by dressing like a teenager is nothing .... of ridiculous.
    Fortunately, our hotel was just a .... walk from the beach.

    | 26 | |

27 Since our sales have fallen recently, we'll be lucky if the company manages to .... even this year.
    You'll .... Jane's heart if you tell her that our holiday has had to be cancelled.
    Many drivers tend to .... the speed limit on this long, straight stretch of road.

    | 27 | |

28 A top managerial post will certainly .... you with a challenge.
    Henry's main ambition is to .... his own TV show.
    I think they should .... Albert with something better than a gold watch on his retirement after forty years' service to the firm.

    | 28 | |

29 Walking through the forest, I had an .... feeling that I was being watched.
    Apart from the .... cold spell, last winter was remarkably mild.
    We can't divide the cakes equally between us if there's an .... number of them.

    | 29 | |

30 The hotel we stayed in didn't .... any resemblance to the one in the holiday brochure photographs.
    As you've got no choice in the matter, you'll just have to grin and .... it.
    Not being a person to .... a grudge, he'll soon forgive you for borrowing his car without permission.

    | 30 | |

31 A serious ankle injury forced the sprinter to .... from the event.
    As a rule, she prefers to go to the bank on Tuesday to .... the money she needs for the week.
    The couple decided to .... their offer for the house after they had read the surveyor's report.

    | 31 | |

Test One

Part 4

For questions **32-39**, complete the second sentence so that it has a similar meaning to the first sentence, using the word given. **Do not change the word given**. You must use between **three** and **eight** words, including the word given. Here is an example (**0**).

Example:

0 We turn on the heating less often because the price of the electricity has gone up.
due
We don't turn on the heating so often .... the price of electricity.

| due to an increase in |

32 The witnesses' evidence didn't give a clear picture of the events at the party.
shed
The witnesses' evidence failed .... had happened at the party.

33 I don't want you to mention our last project at the meeting.
rather
I .... up our last project at the meeting.

34 The president must sign the contract for it to be valid.
considered
The contract cannot .... appears on it.

35 Because of the strike David has been forced to close two of his shops.
resulted
The strike .... two of David's shops.

36 They always shout at each other when they discuss money.
incapable
They .... at each other.

37 George is determined to change his ways and stop lying.
leaf
George is going to .... lie to anyone again.

38 My sociology lecturer always knows what to say in every situation.
loss
My sociology lecturer .... words, whatever the situation.

39 It's a foregone conclusion that Serena will do her best to pass the exams.
goes
It .... every effort to pass her exams.

Paper 3: Use of English

Part 5

For questions **40-44**, read the following texts on genetically modified products. For questions **40-43**, answer with a word or short phrase. You do not need to write complete sentences. For question **44**, write a summary according to the instructions given.

> If you believe that the use of plastic corks in wine bottles was an innovation that went too far, perhaps you had better stop reading now because winemakers have their eye on another technological development that will leave traditionalists spluttering into their claret: genetic modification. All over the world, molecular biologists are tinkering with DNA to find ways to improve the quality of wine.
>
> 5 Already they can do wonders. They can conjure up rare flavours and aromas and add body and complexity to bog-standard plonk. Gene technology can also eliminate the compounds that can make wine taste like sweaty socks, and even get rid of those nasties that give you a bad head in the morning.
>
> Yet, despite the possibilities, winemakers are reluctant to be associated with genetic engineering and it is easy to see why. Wine trades heavily on its image as a traditional product and winemakers cling on
> 10 for dear life to their *terroir* – the blend of soil, climate and skill that gives wine its mystical qualities. No one wants genetic engineers trampling all over that. Winemakers are also scared stiff of the public. Consumers do not like the idea of genetically-modified products, and it would be a foolish winemaker who tried to force it down their throats.
>
> On the quiet, however, winemakers appear to be very interested in the potential of genetic engineering.
> 15 Disease-resistant vines, for example, would help in the fight against devastating infections such as Pierce's disease. But when it comes to quality improvements, only a little attention has been focused on the vine itself. Vines are difficult to engineer and the biological processes that control grape quality are poorly understood.

40 What does the writer imply about molecular biologists by using the word 'tinkering' in line 4?

....

41 What balance must the winemakers strike?

....

A simple sugar has come to the rescue of poor farmers whose soils are too salty, drought-ridden or cold to support crops. The sugar in question is called trehalose, which already enables a hardy desert plant, the so-called 'resurrection plant' to spring back to life when rain arrives. Now, with the help of a pair of genes borrowed from a bacterium, biotechnologists have found a way of altering rice so that it makes its own
5   trehalose.

Every year, millions of hectares of crops are lost through drought or soil salinity. To produce a plant that survives in such conditions, basmati rice was equipped with two genes from *Escherichia coli* that produce trehalose. The sugar is thought to protect plants growing in salty, dry and cold conditions by stabilising proteins and helping to maintain the balance of nutrients and minerals vital for photosynthesis. Previous
10 attempts to engineer plants to make their own trehalose failed miserably, with plants ending up shrivelled.

This time, however, unlike past attempts which kept the trehalose genes turned on throughout the plant at all times, the rice was provided with a genetic switch to activate the sugar-producing genes. So the genes are turned on only when the plant is stressed by a lack of water, for example. In trials the genetically-modified rice survived easily in conditions that killed ordinary rice. The growth rates and
15 weights of the altered rice plants were just 20 per cent below normal when they were exposed to salty, cold or dry conditions. Unaltered plants died or at best struggled to grow at 20 to 30 per cent of their normal rates.

42   Explain in your own words how basmati rice was made to withstand severe conditions.
....

43   What is the purpose of the figures given at the end of the text?
....

44   In a paragraph of between **50 and 70** words, summarise **in your own words as far as possible**, the changes that can be brought about to crops and their products by genetically modifying them.

....
....
....
....
....
....

Test One

Paper 4: Listening

An in-depth look

The **Listening** paper is made up of **four** recordings each with a different task type for you to complete. The texts are all from authentic sources and may be interviews, documentary features, radio plays, informal conversations, lectures, monologues, three way conversations, etc. The task types may include sentence completion, multiple-choice, or deciding which speaker said what and whether the speakers agreed. These tasks can be divided into 'productive' where you have to give a written response to a prompt and 'objective' where you have to choose from a number of alternatives.

THE PRODUCTIVE TASK

Here you have to complete sentences with information from the text. The sentences provide a summary of the main ideas spoken in the text and could include stated opinion as well as direct information. Only single words or short phrases are required to complete the sentence. The words in the gaps will not differ from those heard on the cassette. Correct spelling is required.

OBJECTIVE TASKS

The most common of these tasks is multiple-choice. This type of exercise tests your ability to distinguish between what was said and what was not said, as well as the attitudes and opinions of the speakers. Other tasks include those where two or three alternatives are offered. The text will usually be of a more conversational nature and may focus on the attitudes and opinions of the speakers, on who did or did not say what or on whether the speakers are in agreement on certain points.

General notes

Each piece is heard twice. Passages may contain a variety of accents and background noises may occur at the beginning to set the scene. The Listening paper has 28 questions and lasts approximately 40 minutes.

You answer directly onto your question paper and have five minutes at the end to transfer your answers to a separate answer sheet in pencil. One mark is given for each correct answer and this is scaled up to a mark out of forty. You need 60% to guarantee passing this paper.

Exam technique

In real life, you listen for a reason and generally because you want to, whether you are listening to a friend, the television, an overheard conversation on the bus or to your parents. In a listening exam, you are listening because you have to and you have no idea what you are going to be listening to until the cassette starts. Therefore it is essential to read through each part before the recording starts. As soon as the invigilator informs you that you can look at the question paper, start reading Part 1. You will always be given time to do this, between thirty seconds and one minute, but commence reading as soon as you can, so that you have some idea what you will be listening to and what you should be listening for.

When you hear Part 1 for the first time, answer as many questions as you can. On the second listening, check your answers and complete anything you missed the first time. After attempting to answer all the questions, leave Part 1 and start reading Part 2. Do not sit puzzling over an answer in the first part. If you do, you will not have time to read the second part through and might miss the beginning of the second listening. When Part 2 has played twice, start reading Part 3 and so on.

Try to answer as many questions as possible during the first listening. This gives you the opportunity to relax a little when the piece is played a second time, check your answers and answer anything you were not sure about the first time.

When you transfer your answers to the answer sheet, be careful to write them next to the correct number. Check your spelling and try to guess the answers to any questions you could not answer during that part of the exam. Remember to use pencil on the answer sheet.

Test One

Part 1

You will hear four different extracts. For questions **1-8**, choose the answer (**A**, **B**, or **C**) which fits best according to what you hear. There are two questions for each extract.

Extract One

You hear a man talking about his hobby, marquetry.

1 What gives the man particular pleasure?
    A   buying woods from different countries
    B   handling various woods
    C   collecting different veneers

2 Why does the man recommend buying a starter kit?
    A   to learn about veneers
    B   to avoid buying extra paint
    C   to save money

Extract Two

You hear two friends talking about a drunken driver.

3 What is the woman's attitude towards the driver?
    A   understanding
    B   unsympathetic
    C   tolerant

4 What is the male speaker's view of the actions of the police?
    A   They had acted fairly.
    B   They had been wrong in stopping the driver.
    C   They had acted too harshly.

Extract Three

You hear a woman talking about the town where she lives.

5 What local feature does she find especially attractive?
    A   the mixture of old and new buildings
    B   the fake timbered buildings
    C   the ultra-modern shops

6 What does she say about living in Chester?
    A   She would like to move.
    B   It lacks some amenities.
    C   She has no plans to leave.

Extract Four

You hear an artist talking about his work.

7 What does his work convey?
    A   his private feelings
    B   his personal opinions
    C   his ambitions

8 What is his attitude towards the work he produces?
    A   insecure
    B   confident
    C   embarrassed

Test One

Paper 4: Listening

Part 2

You will hear a radio report about Fair Trade organisations. For questions **9-17**, complete the sentences with a word or short phrase.

A _____ **9** wage is enough to pay for accommodation, meals, education and health needs.

Fair Trade Organisations reduce costs and return a larger proportion of the _____ **10** price to the producers.

Paying more money to the workers doesn't necessarily mean that the consumer has to _____ **11** for a product.

Fair Trade organisations are primarily interested in working with _____ **12** as well as associations owned by the workers and cooperatives.

Working together means that workers can obtain better _____ **13** for their products.

In democratically-run organisations, working conditions are safe and _____ **14**.

Consumers need to understand what the _____ **15** costs of cheaper products are.

Eventually, Fair Trade organisations hope to remove _____ **16** in world trade.

_____ **17** selling to Fair Trade organisations receive a higher percentage of the profits.

Part 3

You will hear an interview with two men, Dan Barton and Rick Henderson, who set up their own soft drinks company three years ago. For questions **18-22**, choose the answer (**A**, **B**, **C** or **D**) which fits best according to what you hear.

18   Rick and Dan
  A   thought that the market for fruit drinks was saturated.
  B   had the idea of starting a business when they were at university.
  C   enjoyed immediate success.
  D   started their business on the spur of the moment.

19   Initially, the bank manager
  A   liked their business plan.
  B   needed time to think about lending them money.
  C   agreed to lend them 60% of what they needed.
  D   offered helpful suggestions about the business.

20   Rick and Dan's lowest moment was when
  A   they realised they would not get a bank loan.
  B   the suppliers changed the terms of the agreement.
  C   they realised they had to raise even more money.
  D   the bank manager told them to forget the whole thing.

21   Why does Rick think their drinks are so popular?
  A   Because they are very sweet.
  B   Because they contain preservatives.
  C   Because they are natural.
  D   Because they are made from processed fruit.

22   What do Rick and Dan plan to do in the near future?
  A   Increase their sales.
  B   Change the name of their product.
  C   Market their products more confidently.
  D   Sell their business in a year.

Part 4

You will hear two people, Nick and Maggie, talking about trends in ice skating. For questions **23-28**, decide whether the opinions are expressed by only one of the speakers, or whether the speakers agree.

Write **N** for Nick
       M for Maggie
or   **B** for both, where they agree.

23   Until recently, there has not been enough interest in skating.   ☐ 23

24   It's not always easy to obtain sponsorship as a skater.   ☐ 24

25   Skaters need to have training facilities available almost constantly.   ☐ 25

26   It would be nice if more families chose skating as a leisure activity.   ☐ 26

27   Outdoor skating is helping to change the attitude towards skating.   ☐ 27

28   Speed skaters need special facilities.   ☐ 28

Paper 5: Speaking

An in-depth look

You will be examined in pairs for about nineteen minutes.

You will be assessed throughout the interview on your fluency, grammatical accuracy, vocabulary appropriate to the task, pronunciation and your ability to communicate. There are two examiners: the interlocutor, who both assesses and asks questions, and the assessor, who does not join in the conversation but observes and assesses.

When you meet the examiners, the exam will start immediately with **Part 1**.

Part 1 involves the interlocutor having a conversation with the two candidates. The candidates are asked to give personal information about themselves and to express personal opinions. This part lasts three minutes.

Next, **Part 2** of the exam starts.

In Part 2 you are given a picture sheet to look at and the interlocutor indicates which two pictures you should look at. Then the interlocutor asks a question to promote a discussion between the two candidates. This discussion lasts for one minute. After this, the interlocutor asks a question about all the pictures on the picture sheet, which the candidates have to talk about for three minutes. You must talk about the photographs in the context of the discussion which the interlocutor has promoted; simply describing and comparing the photographs is not enough. All in all, Part 2 lasts four minutes.

Finally, there is **Part 3** of the exam.

Part 3 of the exam is the longest; it lasts twelve minutes. To begin with, each candidate has to speak on their own for about two minutes about a subject. You are given a card on which is written a question and some prompts to give you some ideas about how to answer the question. When candidate A is given a card, candidate B is also given the same card because, once candidate A finishes speaking, candidate B will have to briefly comment on the subject, too. Both candidates are then asked a final question on the subject. The order is then reversed, and candidate B is given a card with a question and prompts. Candidate B has to speak on the subject for two minutes and then candidate A has to briefly comment on the subject. Once again, both candidates are asked a final question about the subject. After this, the interlocutor asks both candidates a number of general questions about the areas covered in Part 3. This lasts four minutes.

You should not be afraid to ask the examiner to repeat something you have not heard or understood. This would be part of a normal, everyday conversation and, as long as you are polite when you ask, you will not be marked down.

Try to use every opportunity you have to speak English, in or outside the classroom. All the above mentioned sections of the interview can be practised in class or with friends. The more you practise, the more confident and relaxed you will be on the day of the actual interview.

Test One

Exam technique

This part of the test requires you to produce long stretches of clear, coherent speech and to perform well in complex and serious discussions. Topics which could cause offence or start an argument, such as those involving a political or religious matter, will not be used.

All components of the interview can be practised inside or outside the classroom, but this does not mean that you should prepare answers. If you do, you will sound unnatural and the examiner will know what is happening. However, you can prepare yourself by looking at the list of most common topics and learning some relevant vocabulary.

When referring to photographs, remember to use the present continuous, as any action in a photograph is still taking place, regardless of when the picture was taken. When comparing and contrasting, remember to use appropriate language, such as *compared to, in comparison with, conversely, however, in contrast, likewise, equally,* etc.

You are being assessed throughout the interview on your language skills, not your personality, intelligence, knowledge of the world or your opinions. Seize the opportunity to show how well you can communicate.

You cannot prepare for this exam just by answering questions in class. You need to take advantage of every chance that comes along to speak English – with friends, your teacher, tourists and so on. Once you start, you will be surprised at how easy it is and how many people want to communicate with you in English.

One of the most important skills you can develop for this part of the exam is taking initiative. If the examiner asks you a question which only takes a few seconds to answer, try to find things to say on the subject for the rest of the specified time. When speaking to your partner, you should be able to help steer the conversation if you see he or she is having difficulty thinking of something to say.

Test One — Paper 5: Speaking

Part 1

- How do you spend your free time?
- What facilities are there for young people in your area?
- What things would you like to change about the area where you live?
- Which other countries would you consider living in, and why?
- What plans do you have for the next five years?
- How important do you think English will be to you in the future?
- Apart from English, what other skills will be important to you in the future?

Part 2

Here are some pictures of different ways of travelling to work. (Page 170)

a   In this part of the test you are going to do something together. First look at pictures A and B and talk together about how the people who are travelling might be feeling. Discuss which of the two transport options is preferable. You have about one minute for this.

b   Now look at all the pictures. I'd like you to imagine the government is about to launch a campaign to encourage people to leave their cars at home and use public transport more frequently.

Talk together about each of the pictures and decide which picture would be best for the posters to accompany the government campaign. You have three minutes to talk about this.

Part 3

In this part of the test you are going to talk on your own for about two minutes. You need to listen while your partner is speaking because you'll be asked to comment afterwards.

I'm going to give you a card with a question on it and I'd like you to say what you think. There are some ideas on the card for you to use if you like.

Candidate A, here is your card. You have about two minutes to talk.

Prompt Card A

> What should rich nations do to help countries hit by famine or drought?
> - financial aid / volunteers
> - allocation of resources
> - political difficulties

Candidate B, Is there anything you would like to add? (one minute)
Candidates A and **B**, how can we encourage more people to do voluntary work? (one minute)

Test One

Candidate B, look at your card. You have about two minutes to tell us what you think. There are some ideas on the card for you to use if you like.

Prompt Card B

> What can be done to solve the problem of homelessness in large cities?
> - cheaper accommodation
> - welfare benefits
> - job opportunities

Candidate A, what do you think? (one minute)
Candidates A and B, has everybody got a right to adequate accommodation? (one minute)

Both candidates: Now, to finish the test, we're going to talk about basic human rights. (four minutes)

- What do you feel are the basic rights to which every individual is entitled?
- What rights are especially important for children and young people?
- Should governments try to decrease the gap between rich and poor people?
- What is more important, basic health care or ensuring everybody has an education? Why?

Thank you. That is the end of the test.

Test Two — Paper 1: Reading

Hints on multiple choice (Part 2)

This consists of four short texts. After each text there are two four-option multiple choice questions.

To answer the questions which follow each passage, read the text carefully. Understanding every single word is not necessary. To help yourself cope with the unknown vocabulary you will probably encounter in the exam, you need to practise deducing the meaning of unknown words from the context.

The distractors employed in this type of task are generally statements or words which a) are only partly true or only partly paraphrase something from the text or b) are totally irrelevant. The first kind are more difficult and only after you've more carefully considered them and compared them to the text will you understand why they are wrong.

Often you will be required to read a text critically and be able to distinguish fact from opinion and determine the writer's attitude towards the topic. Give special attention to the first paragraph of a text, as it usually sets the tone for the rest of the text. You will be tested on your understanding of different aspects of the passage, such as its main point or points, the writer's opinion or attitude, the theme or gist of the text and the overall purpose of the passage.

A common type of question in this part is one that asks you about the particular way in which a word is used in the text. Your sensitivity to the language is being tested, as well as your ability to understand the writer's attitude to the subject, either in the narrower context in which the word is being used or in the text as a whole.

Test Two

Part 1

For questions 1-18, read the three texts below and decide which answer (**A**, **B**, **C**, or **D**) best fits each gap.

ADVERTISING AND THE MEDIA

There are four companies (NBC, CBS, ABC and Fox) in the top tier of America's national TV networks and they, like the vast majority of media companies, are at the mercy of the ebb and (1) .... of advertising revenue for their very survival. As a result, there is (2) .... competition to secure a market share of viewers that will (3) .... a good state of financial health, keep the shareholders happy and ultimately allow employees to retain their jobs.

Advertising (4) .... are set according to the degree of popularity of the programme during which the commercial is shown. This means that in order to stay financially healthy, the TV networks have to attract and keep viewers by providing them with (5) .... hits. When a show is popular, everyone is content but if its popularity (6) ...., it is likely to be scrapped. The problem then is one of replacement, as launching new shows is a high-risk venture.

1	A	flow	B	run	C	go	D	wane
2	A	rival	B	violent	C	fierce	D	wild
3	A	hold	B	maintain	C	keep	D	stay
4	A	rates	B	ratios	C	proportions	D	levels
5	A	top	B	best	C	smash	D	leading
6	A	slows	B	dims	C	fades	D	weakens

FOOD FOR THOUGHT

Since young school children spend a significant proportion of their day at school, it can be a headache for parents to make sure their (7) .... eat properly while they are there. Their dilemma stems from the fact that while it is highly recommended children should eat five daily (8) .... of fruit and vegetables, they almost invariably opt for junk food instead. Some schools which have become aware of this have made changes to their menu and now provide healthy salad alternatives in their canteens. However, these are often prepared hours (9) .... and after sitting under lights for most of the morning, (10) .... the appearance of anything but an appetising dish.

So, the only solution that very often remains open to parents is that of providing their kids with a (11) .... lunch and keeping their fingers (12) .... that they will not return home with their food untouched.

7	A	siblings	B	offspring	C	spouses	D	kin
8	A	sittings	B	courses	C	dishes	D	helpings
9	A	beforehand	B	advance	C	previous	D	prior
10	A	take on	B	come across	C	send out	D	give over
11	A	set	B	boxed	C	wrapped	D	packed
12	A	crossed	B	tied	C	locked	D	folded

INSECTS

For many people the sight of just a single cockroach in the kitchen is enough to make their skin (13) .... . However, the insects that are visible do not (14) .... the greatest threat to humans. There are several unseen species of insects that are attracted to us for our blood and, while they are unobtrusively drinking it, transmit (15) .... diseases into our systems. Another less direct threat comes in the form of the locust, which devours crops in (16) .... that can contain up to 40 billion insects resembling black clouds up to one kilometre wide.

Given our deep-rooted loathing of insects, it may come as a surprise to learn that the burying beetle has been (17) .... as an endangered species which actually has its own reserve in Rhode Island. Despite our natural aversion to insects, it seems that we are able to (18) .... our instinctive antipathy towards them for the sake of the environment.

13	A	wrinkle	B	creep	C	crawl	D	tingle
14	A	pose	B	inflict	C	incite	D	strike
15	A	grave	B	lethal	C	mortal	D	deadly
16	A	shoals	B	swarms	C	herds	D	packs
17	A	considered	B	classed	C	known	D	called
18	A	disregard	B	decline	C	discard	D	spurn

37

Paper 1: Reading

Part 2

You are going to read four extracts which are all concerned in some way with work. For questions **19-26**, choose the answer (**A**, **B**, **C** or **D**) which you think fits best according to the text.

Advertisement for a job
Physicist/Engineer

NPL is the UK's national standards laboratory. We develop state-of-the-art physical measurement technologies. Our research is vital to improving quality of life in connection with medical advances and the environment.

This is an opportunity to participate in a prestigious project of international importance aimed at the ultimate realisation of a new unit of mass, based on quantum principles.

We require a graduate with a minimum upper second-class degree in physics or engineering, good practical skills, and the enthusiasm and long-term commitment needed to contribute to the success of this project.

The successful candidate will join a small team involved in the development, operation and maintenance of the watt balance.

The work will involve electronics, computing and a range of high accuracy electrical, optical and mechanical measurement techniques. There will be ample opportunity for further development.

19 The advertisement states that the employer
   A is in the forefront of their field.
   B is part of a global network of companies.
   C is a leading pharmaceutical company.
   D is principally concerned with reducing pollution.

20 What is the aim of the project mentioned?
   A to gain prestige for the company
   B to maintain the standard of excellence set by the company
   C to develop a new standard for measuring quantities of matter
   D to provide support for an international team of physicists

Extract from a striking firefighter's diary
Friday 22 November

I'm up at 6.30 am and head straight to the TV room to get the latest news. All the news stations report the strike is going ahead. The bells go off at 7 am, a call to a 'fire all out'. Someone has fallen asleep and left some cooking on. Talk to the occupant about fire safety, leaving leaflets on the importance of smoke alarms. Back at the station, the news channels are reporting that once again the Government has intervened at the last moment, when it looked as if the union and the employers were within a hair's breadth of an agreement. The union position has shifted dramatically from 40 per cent with no strings attached to 16 per cent and an agreement in principle to discuss modernisation that, combined with the right pay formula, would be enough to end this strike and give the public the professional fire service they deserve.

We are all distressed at the thought of leaving the public, which includes our families and friends, without the fire and emergency cover they deserve, but the union and the employers are pointing the finger firmly at the door of the Government.

At 9 am the mobilising system announces the changes of watch, the red doors rattle open and we walk out together, knowing we will all walk back together when the Government has come to its senses. Someone has lit the brazier and ON STRIKE – NOT IN SERVICE signs have gone up.

21 What does the writer say about the strike?
   A Nobody expected it to be called.
   B The public are indifferent towards it.
   C It should have gone ahead earlier.
   D It was almost averted.

22 What is inferred about the attitude of the Government?
   A It has not been consistent.
   B It is irrational.
   C It is disrespectful.
   D It shows a lack of confidence.

BIG FIRM WITH A SMALL IMAGE

No one would ever imagine that John Timpson's family shoe-repairing and key-cutting business is a front runner in the corporate image stakes. It's based in a suburb of Manchester and is distinctly uncharismatic. In the age of computers and electronic media, Timpson's newest product, launched a few weeks ago, is a range of rubber stamps.

Until recently, landlords have generally had a sniffy attitude about letting Timpson rent their premises. All that din cutting keys and hammering on shoe soles made them turn up their noses.

Today the story is very different. Timpson is a respected leader in the corporate image contest. Twice now the company has achieved runaway success in one of the most valued assessments of business performance: *The Sunday Times 100 Best Companies to Work For*.

Timpson came sixth in this year's poll, won by the Asda supermarket group with Microsoft as a runner-up. Last year Timpson had done even better, coming fourth, but in a poll that covered only 50 companies.

Timpson who runs the business's 330 branches, including four new ones that have opened in the last month, says he was 'surprised and delighted' with the fourth place, but this year's result has transformed the company's fortunes.

Indeed, with one or two exceptions such as Richer Sounds, few of the corporate minnows have made it to the list and Timpson has certainly earned its spurs getting there.

23 Landlords were reluctant to rent their premises to Timpson because
   A the company was strictly low-tech.
   B his business generated too much noise.
   C Timpson often damaged rented property.
   D there was no guarantee the rent would be paid on time.

24 Which phrase indicates that Timpson's recent recognition has been deserved?
   A respected leader (paragraph 3)
   B runaway success (paragraph 3)
   C transformed the company's fortunes (paragraph 5)
   D earned its spurs (last paragraph)

BUSINESS AS USUAL

It's that time of year again. Ho, ho, ho and all that jazz. But not for footballers. 25th December is like any other day if you play the game for a living. They barely have time to decide where to position the stationmaster on their new train set before they have to drag themselves away and lace up their boots on the training ground. During my playing career, I would wake up early and just have enough time to open presents with my children before I waved goodbye. They were too young to question why I was going out and, anyway, they were only too glad to be left alone to play with their new toys.

Training sessions tended to be lighter and shorter because the players and staff didn't want to be there. Some players thought they would engender some festive spirit, admittedly small, by wearing Santa Claus hats. Once at Gillingham, we trained in a foot of snow. It was like running in quicksand and I'd never felt so tired. Still, we had a snowball fight and made a snowman, complete with hat. Another year, the club asked me to dress up as Santa Claus for a 'Guess the player' competition on a TV programme.

Most people in life would feel pretty disgruntled if they had to work on 25th December and it's true there were always one or two grumbles about training, but most players appreciated it was our job and we were rewarded well for the necessary sacrifice. It's ironic that footballers, so often associated with having a good time and drinking, are at their most professional at a time when the rest of the country eat and drink themselves stupid.

25 On 25th December, professional footballers
   A very often turned up late for training.
   B always suffered from exhaustion.
   C usually complained bitterly about their misfortune.
   D would reluctantly leave home.

26 The tone of the extract is
   A impersonal.
   B light-hearted.
   C resentful.
   D emotional.

Paper 1: Reading

Part 3

You are going to read an article about a novel and its author. Seven paragraphs have been removed from the article. Choose from the paragraphs **A–H** the one which best fits each gap (**27–33**). There is one extra paragraph which you do not need to use.

The man named C and the woman named N have never actually met. They only know each other by their pen names. C isn't sure how old N is, or what she looks like. N is equally in the dark about C. But they have a crush on each other, and they talk online every day.

27

Wired Love: A romance of dots and dashes came out in the spring of 1879, the first and perhaps only book about a long-distance romance conducted by means of the telegraph – or what has been aptly termed 'The Victorian Internet'. Written by the previously unknown Ella Cheever Thayer, *Wired Love*'s Manhatten publisher trumpeted it as 'a bright little telegraphic novel' that told 'the old, old story – in a new way.'

28

When the real C moves to Nattie's town, they are terribly shy of each other. 'I had more of your company on the wire,' Nattie complains. So they string telegraph wire between their apartments, and stay up half the night wiring each other. It might as well have been the 21st century.

29

Thayer herself was a trained telegraph operator. Born in 1849 in Saugus, Massachusetts, the first child of apothecary George Thayer and teacher Mary Cheever, Thayer was hit hard by her father's death in 1863. Thayer and her sister Mary eventually moved to Boston to seek work. Mary became a teacher and Thayer took up work as a telegrapher at the Brunswick Hotel, one of the finest in the city.

30

Perhaps to satisfy her ambition, Thayer turned to writing. She had already published fiction in children's magazines after an 1869 debut with an inauspicious poem in a pamphlet published by her piano teacher. But nobody could have expected the extraordinary novel that she wrote while working at the Brunswick Hotel.

31

Even more extraordinary is Thayer's prediction of wireless love. 'We will soon be able to do everything by electricity. Perhaps some genius will invent something for the special use of lovers. Something, for instance, to carry in their pockets, so when they are far away from each other, and pine for a sound of "That beloved voice", they will only have to take up this electrical apparatus, put it to their ears and be happy. Ah! Blissful lovers of the future!'

32

Thayer never published another book. And yet there are many other 'Wired Loves' on our shelves now. The explosive growth of e-mail generated a burst of fiction in the late 1990s that tapped into similar ideas: from Nan McCarthy's trilogy *Crash, Chat and Connect* (1996), to Astro Teller's *Exegisis* (1997) and Matt Beaumont's *E* (2000). Even mainstream fare such as Helen Fielding's *You've Got Mail* got in on the act. E-mail is now a humdrum part of everyday life, like the telephone, the telegraph and the penny post before it. But when the 'next big thing' comes along, short-lived fictional offspring will be sure to follow.

33

Wired Love has now been out of print for well over a century. There is not even a copy in the libraries at Saugus and Boston. No picture of America's first telegraphic novelist and first suffragette playwright is known to exist and there is no commemorative plaque in her hometown. The Hotel Brunswick is no more.

A After *Wired Love*, Thayer moved on to an even bolder vision of the future. Her next work, *The Lords of Creation*, was America's first suffragist play. It was published in 1883, but never performed.

B In those days, this occupation offered a great opportunity to young women. Learning Morse was rather like learning to type or using Microsoft Office. Laura Otis of Hofstra University in New York, who studied Thayer's work for her book *Networking*, concurs: 'Telegraphy provided exhilarating opportunities for women when there were few jobs available, and gave them the dignity of earning an income.' But the limited opportunities women had for advancement must have chafed on the ambitious Thayer. Otis points out that when Henry James needed a resentful worker for his novella *In the Cage*, he chose a woman telegrapher.

C Yet Thayer's story was grounded in Victorian reality. Men and women alike worked as telegraph operators, with predictable results: at least one wedding was conducted over the wires. *Electrical World* magazine even warned of 'the dangers of wired love'. When one Brooklyn woman used a telegraph to carry on a secret affair with a married man, her father 'threatened to blow her brains out, and she therefore had him arrested,' the magazine reported.

D *Wired Love* came out at the high-water mark of telegraphy. 'There was probably only a small window where such a novel would have been, er, novel,' says Tom Standage, author and science writer for the *Economist*. Indeed, the book's characters already marvel over the latest novelty – the telephone – and speculate about faxes. 'Isn't there a – a something – a fac simile arrangement?' one character asks.

E But there is one surviving monument to her life. The Boston apartment where she wrote *Wired Love*, a three-storey brick building at 283 Shawmut Avenue, is still standing.

F The initials stand for Nattie and Clem and she can't even be sure C is a man. She admits that her online romance is almost certainly hopeless. 'In all probability, we will never meet. I think I would be dreadfully embarrassed if we did. Face to face we would really be strangers to each other.' It's the old story about online romance, but it's older than you think. Much older.

G The genre's godmother remains a shadowy literary figure. Thayer went on to children's magazine hack work, and then settled into newspaper work in Boston. She never married, but stayed close to her sister in the city. Two decades after her last book she still defiantly listed her occupation as 'author' in the Boston directory. But what little reputation she had as an author or journalist was quickly forgotten. When she died in 1925, not a single Boston newspaper bothered to run a death notice for their late colleague.

H Equal parts old-fashioned romance and newfangled novel, *Wired Love* follows the infatuation of two telegraph operators in unspecified American frontier towns. Other operators listen in and ridicule them. 'Picture a hippopotamus and an elephant,' one interloper snipes when C wonders what N looks like. At one point Nattie is even deceived by an impostor of C, sporting bear-greased hair, stinking cologne, cheap jewellery and 'teeth all at variance with each other'.

Test Two — Paper 1: Reading

Part 4

You are going to read an extract from an article on language. For questions **34-40**, choose the answer (**A**, **B**, **C**, or **D**) which you think fits best according to the text.

YOU ARE WHAT YOU SPEAK

Does the language you speak influence the way you think? Does it help define your world view? Anyone who has tried to master a foreign tongue has at least considered the possibility. As have those who have ever had a close foreign friend.

At first glance, the idea that language influences thought seems perfectly plausible. Conveying even simple messages requires that you make completely different observations depending on your language. Imagine being asked to count some pens on a table. As an English speaker, you only have to count them and give the number. Let's say there are eleven. But a Russian also has to consider what gender the pens are (neuter) and then use the neuter form of the word for eleven. And a Japanese speaker has to take into account their shape (long and cylindrical) as well, and use the word for eleven designated for items of that form.

On the other hand, surely pens are just pens, no matter what your language compels you to specify about them. Little linguistic peculiarities, though amusing, don't change the objective world we are describing. So how can they alter the way we think?

Scientists and philosophers have been grappling with this thorny question for centuries. There have always been those who argue that our picture of the universe depends on our native tongue. Since the 1960s, however, with the ascent of thinkers like Noam Chomsky and a host of cognitive scientists, the consensus has been that linguistic differences don't really matter, that language is a universal human trait and that our ability to talk to one another owes more to our shared genetics than to our varying cultures. But now the pendulum is beginning to swing the other way as psychologists re-examine the question.

The new generation of scientists is not convinced that language is innate and hard-wired into our brain. 'Language is not just notation,' says Dan Slobin of the University of California. 'The brain is shaped by experience.' Slobin and others say that small, even apparently insignificant differences between languages do affect the way speakers perceive the world. 'Some people argue that language just changes what you attend to,' says Lera Boroditsky of the Massachusetts Institute of Technology. 'But what you attend to changes what you encode and remember.'

This is what Slobin calls 'thinking for speaking' and he argues that it can have a huge impact on what we deem important. For instance, about a third of the world's languages describe location in 'absolute' terms: speakers of many Pacific Island languages would say 'north of the tree' or 'seaward from the tree' rather than 'beside the tree', as we might in English. In these languages, you always need to know where you are in relation to fixed external reference points, says Slobin. 'Even when you are in a dark windowless room, or travelling on a bus in the dark,' he says, 'you must know your location relative to the fixed points in order to talk about events and locations.' So, even if you didn't use the word 'north' in conversation, you would always know where it was.

Whether your language emphasises an object's shape, substance or function also seems to affect your relationship with the world, according to John Lucy, a researcher at the Max Planck Institute for Psycholinguistics. He has compared American English with Yucatec Maya, spoken in Mexico's Yucatan Peninsula. Among the many differences between the two languages is the way objects are classified. In English, shape is implicit in many nouns. We think in terms of discrete objects; and it is only when we want to quantify amorphous things like sugar that we employ units such as 'cube' or 'cup'. But in Yucatec, objects tend to be defined by separate words that describe shape. So, for example, a 'short flat leather' is a wallet. Likewise, 'long banana' describes the fruit, while 'flat banana' means banana leaf and a 'seated banana' is a banana tree.

Boroditsky also argues that even artificial classification systems, such as gender, can be important. The word 'sun' is neutral in Russian, feminine in German and masculine in Spanish. Some psychologists claim that these inconsistencies suggest gender is just a meaningless tag, but Boroditsky disagrees. 'To construct sentences in these languages,' she says, 'involves thinking about gender – even if it's arbitrary – thousands of times every day.'

To test how this affects the way people think, she presented Spanish and German-speaking volunteers with nouns that happened to have opposite genders in their native tongues. 'Key', for instance, is feminine in Spanish and masculine in German and 'bridge' is masculine in Spanish and feminine in German. Boroditsky asked the volunteers to come up with adjectives – in English – to describe these items. German speakers described keys as 'awkward', 'worn', 'jagged' and 'serrated', while Spanish speakers saw them as 'little', 'lovely', 'magic' and 'intricate'. To Germans, bridges were 'awesome', 'fragile', 'beautiful' and 'elegant', whereas Spanish speakers considered them 'big', 'solid', 'dangerous', 'strong' and 'sturdy'.

34 A positive answer to the questions in the first paragraph would most probably be given by
  A a student at an advanced stage of foreign language learning.
  B a person who has worked abroad but has not learned a second language.
  C someone who has been involved in an intimate relationship with a foreigner.
  D a foreigner who has many close friends.

35 The question in paragraph 4 is described as 'thorny' because
  A nobody knows the answer.
  B the answer varies according to the language analysed.
  C it has only recently been considered important.
  D it is difficult to answer.

36 What is the purpose of the reference to 'the pendulum'? (paragraph 4)
  A to show that genetic differences among races are insignificant
  B to suggest that Chomsky's theory is no longer accepted as correct
  C to suggest that human speech patterns are hereditary
  D to state that cultural differences account for linguistic differences

37 According to Lera Boroditsky, what a person pays closest attention to reflects their
  A linguistic prowess.
  B thought processes.
  C powers of observation.
  D intellectual abilities.

38 In a typical Pacific Island language
  A orientation is vitally important.
  B recognition of every type of vegetation is essential.
  C descriptions of journeys are relatively brief.
  D north is always the point of reference.

39 According to John Lucy, English speakers think of objects as
  A needing units of measurement.
  B not having a clear shape.
  C separate and distinct.
  D masculine or feminine.

40 The presence of gender in a language
  A leads to confusion for native English speakers.
  B determines the way complex sentences are constructed.
  C affects the way objects are perceived.
  D determines the order in which adjectives appear.

Test Two — Paper 2: Writing

Part 1

You must answer this question. Write your answer in **300-350** words in an appropriate style.

1 You have read the extract below as part of a series of newspaper articles on addiction. Readers were asked to send in their opinions. You decide to write a letter responding to the points raised and expressing your own views.

> At a time when so many families face financial difficulties, gambling is being promoted with the promise of huge sums of money for the lucky winners. This has caused further financial hardship for people spending money they can ill afford to lose in their quest for the impossible dream, a state of affairs which has often led to disaster for both the gamblers and their families. Isn't it time something was done to remedy the situation?

Write your **letter**. Do not write any postal addresses.

Part 2

Write an answer to one of the questions **2-4** in this part. Write your answer in **300-350** words in an appropriate style.

2 A local careers office publishes a monthly magazine for students. The editor of the magazine has invited local business people to contribute articles describing their working day. You have decided to write an article for the magazine describing your normal working day.

   Write your **article**.

3 As part of a training programme, you have recently completed a two-week course at a local college. Write a letter to the course director stating which aspects of the course were satisfactory and those which were disappointing. Suggest what could be done to improve this part of the training programme and include any comments about the accommodation that was provided.

   Write your **letter**.

4 You are employed by a company specialising in luxury holidays. You have been asked by the manager to visit a hotel which has recently opened and write a report based on the visit. Depending on your findings, the company may or may not decide to include the new hotel in its luxury holiday brochure.

   Write your **report**.

Hints on writing a report

There is more than one type of report. For example:

- news reports
- assessment reports
- informative reports

A report is normally written for only one person to read in some sort of work or business situation. A report should include the following:

- headings – this enables the reader to find specific information quickly
- facts about an event or a situation that the reader can understand clearly
- formal language
- formal connectors, such as *Firstly, In addition to this, However, A final point*, etc.
- passive voice – impersonal constructions – *'I'* should not be used
- impersonal verbs – *it seems, appears*, etc.
- adverbs such as *surprisingly, predictably*, etc.
- recommendations (if appropriate)

A report should not include contractions such as *I'm, he's*, etc.

Planning a report is very important as your ideas need to be presented clearly.

GENERAL REPORT PLAN

Introduction:	The aim of the report, what information it is based on (personal findings, survey, complaints, etc.), and, if appropriate, who prepared it and for whom.
Main body:	Presentation of the information. Comments or suggestions under suitable paragraph headings.
Conclusion:	A final assessment and/or any recommendations.

Test Two

Paper 3: Use of English

Hints on word formation (Part 2)

In this part of the Use of English paper, you have to complete a short text containing ten gaps. At the end of each line with a gap, there is a word which has to be transformed to provide the missing word.

You must make a new word from the word given which fits both the grammatical structure and the meaning of the sentence.

When you have completed the task, read the whole text through carefully to make sure that it sounds right. Should the nouns you have used be singular or plural? Should the adjectives or adverbs be affirmative or negative?

Bear in mind that you will often have to make more than one change to a word. Eg, you may be given the word *understand* and be expected to come up with *misunderstandings*.

The new word must also be a different part of speech from the one given in the margin. Eg, if you are given a verb, you will have to come up with a noun, adjective or adverb.

Test Two

Part 1

For questions **1-15**, read the text below and think of the word which best fits each space. Use only one word in each space. There is an example at the beginning (**0**).

Example: | 0 | OF |

Doddington Hall Gardens

Five miles south-west (0)......*OF*...... Lincoln lies Doddington Hall, a superb Elizabethan mansion with its historically-important walled gardens. (1) .... most of the gardens around stately homes and period country houses, (2) .... at Doddington Hall reflect changing fashions in landscaping and planting ideas (3) .... the centuries.

What (4) .... Doddington unusual, (5) .... , is that the gardens are still recognisably the (6) .... in structure as when they were laid out in the early part of the 17th century. This is basically (7) .... to Sir John Duval's resistance to the changes advocated by Lancelot 'Capability' Brown and his followers during the 18th century.

Brown and his acolytes thought (8) .... of moving entire villages if they got in the (9) .... of a view. So, they would certainly not have batted an (10) .... as they readily swept (11) .... trees, plants and walls in (12) .... of fashionable 'natural' landscape design. Sir John, on the other (13) .... , remained faithful (14) .... tradition, regularly improving and restoring his 17th-century gardens and maintaining the walls.

His example of careful preservation has been followed (15) .... since, and it has even been suggested that if Sir John were able to visit the house today, 200 years after his death, he would feel instantly at home.

Part 2

For questions **16-25**, read the text below. Use the word given in capitals at the end of some of the lines to form a word that fits in the space in the same line. There is an example at the beginning (**0**).

Example: | 0 | CELEBRATED |

Henry Moore on sculpture

Not only was Henry Moore Britain's most (0) ......*CELEBRATED*...... modern sculptor but he also provided a valuable insight into the art form with which his name has become (16)	CELEBRATE SYNONYM
In his book *Notes on Sculpture*, he seemed to have been somewhat (17) .... by the fact that this particular art form very often remained (18) .... by so many people who were what he called 'form-blind'. This 'condition' prevents the observer from producing the active (19) .... necessary to understand a three-dimensional form, thus making it largely (20) .... It was this gap in communication between the sculptor and the public that he attempted to bridge through his (21) .... notes on how a sculptor thinks and views the world.	SAD APPRECIATE RESPOND COMPREHEND EXPLAIN
According to Henry Moore, a sculptor is able to comprehend form in its full spatial existence by mentally (22) .... it, regardless of size, completely enclosed in the hollow of his hand. As he does this, he (23) .... knows what it looks like from all angles, where its centre of gravity is and what its volume, weight and mass are.	VISUAL INSTINCT
Henry Moore was particularly interested in the use of holes in sculpture. He actually described the first hole made through a piece of stone as a (24) .... He claimed it made the form immediately three-dimensional which, in turn, may have made it much more (25) .... to those suffering from 'form-blindness'.	REVEAL ACCESS

Paper 3: Use of English

Part 3

For questions **26-31**, think of one word only which can be used appropriately in all three sentences. Here is an example (**0**).

Example:

0 The committee's main aim this year is to .... enough money to build two new tennis courts.
   Please .... your hand whenever you want to speak to the teacher.
   My landlord intends to .... my rent by almost 15% next year.

   | 0 | RAISE |

26 You can .... yourself lucky that you weren't fired for speaking so rudely to the supervisor.
    All his hard work will .... for nothing if he doesn't complete the project.
    A poor attendance record at work will certainly .... against you when you apply for another job.

27 They .... to make a large profit on the shares they have bought.
    A female tiger will always .... her ground to protect her cubs.
    Several shops now .... where the old cinema used to be.

28 We normally begin our warm-up exercises by running on the .... for five minutes.
    She had a soft .... for her little niece.
    In my opinion, the perfect .... for a picnic is high on a grassy hill with a wonderful view on all sides.

29 The police do not think there is enough evidence to .... the suspect with murder.
    Since we live outside the village, the local shopkeepers .... us extra when they deliver goods for us.
    The bull took one look at the boys crossing the field and decided to ....

30 Helen's hair is very .... brown, almost blond.
    Doctors usually advise against their patients doing anything but .... work immediately after recovering from surgery.
    A .... sea breeze can make a very hot summer day more pleasant.

31 Only the managing director has the .... to approve expenses of over £1,500.
    Being an .... on primitive religions, he is very often invited to give his expert opinion in documentaries.
    Because the crime was committed in another country, our police force has no .... in the case.

Part 4

For questions **32-39**, complete the second sentence so that it has a similar meaning to the first sentence, using the word given. **Do not change the word given**. You must use between **three** and **eight** words, including the word given. Here is an example (**0**).

Example:

0 The mountaineers tried desperately to reach base camp before nightfall.
   attempt
   The mountaineers .... to base camp before nightfall.

   | made a desperate attempt to get |

32 I haven't had the time to answer George's letter yet.
   round
   I haven't .... to George's letter yet.

33 From what you told John, he thought you would resign.
   impression
   You .... your resignation when you spoke to him.

34 I can't understand how the proposed changes will be beneficial to us.
   fail
   I .... the proposed changes.

35 The manager refuses to talk to the press until the end of the season.
   finished
   Only when .... talk to the press.

36 Although the couple are getting on, they do not need anyone to care for them.
   fend
   The elderly couple .... their age.

37 Henry's colleagues ignored him after he reported one of them for leaving work early.
   shoulder
   Henry .... his colleagues for reporting one of them for leaving work early.

38 Lending Sally so much money was a rather foolish thing to do.
   better
   You should .... Sally so much money.

39 Alligators and crocodiles look very much alike to me.
   tell
   I .... an alligator and a crocodile.

Paper 3: Use of English

Part 5

For questions **40-44**, read the following texts on building a holiday home in Croatia. For questions **40-43**, answer with a word or short phrase. You do not need to write complete sentences. For question **44**, write a summary according to the instructions given.

> For anybody looking to find a seaside plot on which to build their dream home, the Adriatic may provide the perfect choice. Europe's newest holiday destination, Croatia, has a relatively unspoiled coast and some lovely offshore islands that have drawn droves of foreign buyers since 2000, when peace finally returned to the war-stricken Balkans. But although the seemingly endless shoreline might
> 5 appear to offer a cornucopia of opportunities, in reality there are only a few areas worth looking at.
>
> Much of the north coast is sheer rock which was great for 16th-century pirates, but is not so good for modern home-builders. Most people look in south-central Dalmatia and the islands. Generally the islands such as Brac are less costly than the mainland, but there are exceptions. Korcula and Hvar are prettier and more exclusive, but much of their best coastline has already been built on or put under
> 10 conservation orders. These orders may not be sacred, though. The coastal village of Lumbarda on Korcula, for example, is seeking government permission to put more of its coastline into the all-important building zone category.
>
> As far as the mainland is concerned, the Dubrovnik area is particularly popular and correspondingly expensive. Other possibilities include villages like Zaton and Cavtat, but as Croatia is not an EU
> 15 member, it is under no obligation to treat foreign and local buyers equally. Foreigners need a permit to buy land and, while it is virtually automatic in terms of administration, it can take time. More crucially, though, foreign builders are not allowed to erect new buildings on empty land. They can only upgrade or expand existing structures. In addition to this limitation, finding a plot with the right permits can be tricky as local estate agents have a rotten reputation for gliding over planning and multiple-ownership
> 20 difficulties.

40 Which two words in the first paragraph give the impression of large numbers?
....

41 What does the phrase 'may not be sacred' in line 10 imply?
....
....

Test Two

After a decade of painstaking restoration, Dubrovnik, the jewel of Croatia, seems at long last to be on the threshold of a boom. The wounds of the war have almost healed, and the city has never been so carefree and well-heeled. Until recently, most of Croatia's visitors came form Eastern Europe but now more and more wealthy westerners are being drawn by an irresistible combination of clean beaches, sparkling sea, good food and cheap wine. The coastline, one of the most beautiful in the world, is strung with a necklace of sun-soaked and often empty islands, most of which contain plots of land that are ripe for building a dream home.

Dubrovnik and the surrounding area, as one would expect, leads the way in the coming boom. After years of lying empty, hotels and houses have been snapped up and restored with lavish amounts of foreign capital. With enough money it is possible to buy a property from which you can leap into the transparent blue-green Adriatic. The views inland are also impressive, framed by cypresses and the huge walls and fortresses of the city.

The news for prospective home builders is not all good, however, and the revival of the city's fortunes is creating new pressures. Plans are afoot to build large blocks of flats and several other buildings on the steep hillside half a mile away from the city. This will obviously spoil the view inland. On the other front, the frequent arrival of huge cruise liners are playing havoc with the city's medieval sense of scale. The sudden presence of one of these monsters is like having an office block dumped on one's doorstep. Nevertheless, for the time being at least, the place has great potential for a holiday home.

42 In your own words, what are the 'new pressures' referred to in line 14?
....
....

43 What image of cruise liners does the writer create by using the word 'dumped' in line 17?
....

44 In a paragraph of between **50 and 70** words, summarise **in your own words as far as possible**, the problems given in the texts that a foreign home builder in Croatia might face.
....
....
....
....
....
....

Paper 4: Listening

Hints on sentence completion (Part 2)

In Part 2 of the Listening paper, you are asked to note down points of information from the text in response to given prompts. You are required to write a word or short phrase in response to prompts which focus on the main points of the information presented in the text.

You are being tested on your ability to listen for detail, follow the structure of the text and isolate relevant information. Most answers will be short, often single words or noun groups.

As with all types of listening exercise, you must read the given information before you listen so you know what you are listening for and what type of information you will have to complete. Think about the topic and what type of information you may have to put in. Use your general knowledge to help you think about the topic, but only write down what you actually hear. Listen carefully to any times or figures mentioned. Numbers can sound very similar, eg, fifteen and fifty. You will only be required to write what you actually hear on the tape. You are not required to rephrase what you have heard on the tape although you must make sure that what you write fits grammatically in the sentence.

Do not spend too long thinking about what to write for one question as you might then miss the information for the next one. Answer as many questions as you can the first time you hear the tape. On the second playing, focus on listening for what you haven't completed and check what you have already completed.

When you transfer your answers to the answer sheet, do so carefully and remember to check your spelling. Correct spelling is required for this part of the Listening paper.

Make sure that your handwriting is neat as the examiner must be able to read your answer.

Test Two

Part 1

You will hear four different extracts. For questions **1-8**, choose the answer (**A**, **B**, or **C**) which fits best according to what you hear. There are two questions for each extract.

Extract One

You hear a man talking about the harmful effects of caffeine.

1 What was the man's attitude to caffeine before he saw his doctor?
    A   He knew it was harmful.
    B   He didn't realise what damage it could do.
    C   He was anxious about it.

2 How did the man feel when he first gave up caffeine?
    A   He felt healthier.
    B   He wasn't well.
    C   It made his muscles tense and his heart beat faster.

Extract Two

You hear a rally driver being interviewed.

3 What happens to the man once he starts driving?
    A   He tries to control his thoughts.
    B   He thinks only about his driving.
    C   He feels a strong sense of excitement.

4 What did the man think when he'd followed the incorrect instructions?
    A   He was going to die.
    B   He wanted to kill the navigator.
    C   He had wasted time.

Extract Three

You hear a woman talking about cooking.

5 What does the speaker feel about recipes?
    A   They are only a guide to how to cook.
    B   They must be strictly adhered to.
    C   They aren't exciting.

6 The food at the speaker's restaurant is unlikely to appeal to
    A   fans of her cookery books.
    B   people who like it prepared the traditional way.
    C   adventurous people.

Extract Four

You hear two friends talking about cigarette packets.

7 The female speaker claims that in the past
    A   the effects of cigarettes were kept secret.
    B   cigarettes were too strong.
    C   people were not as well-informed about the dangers of smoking.

8 What does the male speaker say about governments?
    A   They make a lot of money from cigarette sales.
    B   They have only just found out how harmful cigarettes can be.
    C   They have a cynical view of smoking and smokers.

Test Two — Paper 4: Listening

Part 2

You will hear a radio report about Global Positioning Systems. For questions **9-17**, complete the sentences with a word or short phrase.

You won't lose your way if you have a GPS receiver and can see the _____ **9**

The Global Positioning System consists of _____ **10** satellites in total.

All the GPS satellites rotate the globe _____ **11** a day.

GP receivers can always get signals from _____ **12** of the satellites.

To find your exact location, look at the _____ **13** on your GPS.

A GPS receiver can follow _____ **14** on a map as you travel.

As well as location on a map, route and speed, the receiver can give your _____ **15** of arrival.

Routes may be fed into a _____ **16** and used again in the future.

It's possible that GPS receivers could be used to stop children _____ **17**

Test Two

Part 3

You will hear an interview with Meg Taylor, who recently carried out some research on the use of CCTV cameras in Britain. For questions **18-22**, choose the answer (**A**, **B**, **C** or **D**) which fits best according to what you hear.

18 What is the consequence of such a high concentration of cameras in cities?
   - **A** Most people are constantly monitored outside their home.
   - **B** People are under surveillance in their own homes.
   - **C** Privacy inside the home is almost extinct.
   - **D** Cameras are everywhere except in restaurants.

19 The number of CCTV cameras per person in Britain is
   - **A** not as high as in the United States.
   - **B** the highest in the world.
   - **C** not as high as people might think.
   - **D** increasing at a faster rate than in the US.

20 Civil Rights campaigners are worried that
   - **A** individuals could begin using CCTV cameras.
   - **B** companies could use these cameras to spy on other companies.
   - **C** the cameras could be used to invade privacy.
   - **D** the usage of the cameras is spreading.

21 Controversially, some firms use CCTV cameras
   - **A** for profit.
   - **B** to monitor meetings.
   - **C** to watch their employees.
   - **D** to prevent theft.

22 Meg's general view is that CCTV cameras
   - **A** are a danger to civil rights.
   - **B** can be abused by vandals.
   - **C** are only useful if they have zoom lenses.
   - **D** are valuable in crime detection.

Part 4

You will hear two people, Fiona and Jamie, talking about the new Park and Ride Scheme in a nearby city. For questions **23-28**, decide whether the opinions are expressed by only one of the speakers, or whether the speakers agree.

Write   **F**   for Fiona
        J   for Jamie
or   **B**   for Both, where they agree.

23 The scheme means that it takes less time to get to the shops.
24 I end up in pain when I go shopping.
25 It would be a good idea to have a place to leave shopping.
26 The buses ought to run every ten minutes.
27 Planners didn't come up with the best possible route.
28 Generally, consumers are pleased with the scheme.

Test Two — Paper 5: Speaking

Part 1

- What do you do? Talk about your work or your studies.
- What career plans do you have?
- Would you ever consider working abroad?
- What sports are you especially keen on?
- How important to you is your social life?
- Do you live with friends or family?
- Would you like to tell us about the house or apartment where you live?

Part 2

Here are some pictures of our surroundings. (page 171)

a In this part of the test you're going to do something together. First, I'd like you to look at pictures A and B and discuss the ways in which the scenes depicted are vulnerable to environmental damage. You have one minute for this.

b Now I'd like you to look at all the pictures. I'd like you to imagine that these photographs are to be included in an environmental magazine. They depict different aspects of our environment that are currently being destroyed in one way or another.

Talk together about which aspect you think is the most important for us to preserve at all costs and how this would be achieved. You have about three minutes to talk about this.

Part 3

In this part of the test you are going to talk on your own for about two minutes. You need to listen while your partner is speaking because you'll be asked to comment afterwards.

I'm going to give you a card with a question on it and I'd like you to say what you think. There are some ideas on the card for you to use if you like.

Candidate A, here is your card.

> **Prompt Card A**
>
> Do you think air travel should be stopped, or at least limited?
> - air/noise pollution
> - increase fares
> - re-siting airports

Candidate B, is there anything you don't agree with? (1 minute)
Candidates A and B, should space travel be stopped until we can find ways of sending rockets into space without harming our environment? (1 minute)

Candidate B, look at your card and say what you think.

> **Prompt Card B**
>
> How can we stop more species of animals becoming endangered?
> - stop hunting
> - strict penalties
> - zoos

Candidate A, is there anything you would like to add? (1 minute)
Candidate A and B, What is your opinion of wildlife parks and nature reserves?

Both candidates: Now to finish the test, we're going to talk about the environment. (4 minutes)

- Do you think governments do enough to protect the environment?
- What more could be done to improve the situation in your country?
- What can you as individuals do to help the environment?
- How confident can we be that our planet will still exist two hundred years from now?

Test Two

Most commonly-asked general questions

- What's the best way of learning a foreign language? (Language school, audio cassettes, television, etc.)

- Why are you learning English and what are your plans for the future? How are you going to use the language?

- What do you do? (This is a common question if the student is older and working.)

- Are you interested in learning about British or American culture? Is English only a qualification to you?

- Which language do you think will be most important in the future?

- How and where do you usually spend your summer holidays/Christmas/Easter?

- Where would your ideal holiday be in the English speaking world? Australia? The United States? Ireland? Great Britain? Jamaica? Why?

- Have you ever visited a country that you prefer to your own? Would you like to live there? How would your lifestyle differ from your present one? Why?

- How do you like to spend your free time? Do you have any hobbies? Do you play any sport?

- Do you have a particular career in mind for the future? What attracts you to this job/profession?

- Do you think children today have too much freedom?

- Where would you most like to visit in the world and why?

- Do you think school holidays are too long?

- How long have you lived in this area? What do you most like or dislike about it? Would you prefer to live elsewhere? Why?

Test Three

Paper 1: Reading

Hints on the gapped text with paragraphs removed (Part 3)

In Part 3 of the reading paper, there is a text of between 800-1100 words. Paragraphs have been removed from the text and placed in a jumbled order after it. You have to decide from where in the text the paragraphs have been taken.

Here you are being tested on how you understand a text. That is, how a text is structured, what cohesive devices are employed and general understanding.

You will need to practise being able to follow the order of a text from the beginning to the end. Being able to spot linking devices is essential.

In order to know where to place a missing paragraph, you must be aware of the internal logic and flow of ideas in a text, ie, a text's coherence. Clues to look out for are the way the beginning of one paragraph may refer back to the preceding one or whether the writer seems to be referring to something for the first time or if they have already referred to it.

Test Three

Part 1

For questions **1-18**, read the three texts below and decide which answer (**A**, **B**, **C**, or **D**) best fits each gap.

TRENDS IN THE PROPERTY MARKET

Ever since property prices in Britain began to rise at previously unseen rates, it has been predicted that they would eventually (1) .... , allowing more young couples to buy their own home. Unfortunately for those first-time buyers, though, the property market has been fuelled by single buyers as they scramble to get on the first (2) .... of the housing ladder. Soaring prices have meant that many prospective buyers, who have been saving for years, have reached the end of their (3) .... as they can now no longer afford to buy the kind of property they had (4) .... their hearts on. The money they have been putting away is now simply inadequate for their needs which means their efforts may have been in (5) .... . To add (6) .... to injury, it has been forecast by leading economists that this dramatic shift towards more and more people buying on their own home is set to continue over the next twenty years.

1	A	level off	B	change down	C	stop off	D	step down
2	A	step	B	pace	C	rung	D	stage
3	A	wits	B	tether	C	line	D	road
4	A	put	B	got	C	set	D	taken
5	A	error	B	vain	C	mistake	D	misjudgement
6	A	provocation	B	damage	C	insult	D	harm

WILDLIFE RESCUE

Although the wildlife rescue centre in Leatherhead, Surrey, is only one of many throughout Europe, it has become the most famous because it is (7) .... on a television channel called 'Animal Planet'. Like all the other centres, the staff at Leatherhead are (8) .... to treating sick, injured, or orphaned wild animals and returning them to the wild after they have been given a (9) .... bill of health. Most rescues result in a successful release, but unfortunately some animals have to be (10) .... . The criterion for deciding whether euthanasia is necessary is the animal's ability to survive in the wild after treatment.

The centre is (11) .... dependent on donations from the (12) .... public so open days are organised in order to raise funds to ensure the centre can continue its valuable work.

7	A	broadcast	B	presented	C	featured	D	characterised
8	A	concentrated	B	assigned	C	appointed	D	dedicated
9	A	new	B	clean	C	pure	D	fresh
10	A	put down	B	turned over	C	passed away	D	taken out
11	A	specifically	B	heavily	C	grossly	D	significantly
12	A	usual	B	regular	C	ordinary	D	general

A SPACE-AGE HOTEL

In a country where 'bigger' inevitably means 'better' and stupendously large luxury hotels are all the (13) .... , a new colossus has sprung up in Manhattan, New York. The Westin's 45-storey façade may not make it imposing in terms of height, but as it is composed of 8000 sheets of glass in ten different colours, it does not fail to catch the eye of passers-by. It has also caught the attention of the press by whom it has been given a mixed reception. On the one hand, it has (14) .... scathing criticism from some journalists who have implied that the architects had taken leave of their (15) .... while working on the plans. On the other hand, it has been (16) .... as a triumph of architectural daring.

As far as the public is concerned, New Yorkers seem to be sitting on the (17) .... , reluctant to take sides in the argument about the building's architectural merits, so it is uncertain what the final verdict will be. One thing, however, is guaranteed: the Westin will remain a (18) .... point for some time to come.

13	A	fashion	B	rage	C	craze	D	mode
14	A	come in for	B	come out with	C	come up with	D	come out in
15	A	minds	B	brains	C	feelings	D	senses
16	A	attributed	B	declared	C	hailed	D	associated
17	A	wall	B	fence	C	side	D	hedge
18	A	discussing	B	telling	C	talking	D	debating

Test Three — Paper 1: Reading

Part 2

You are going to read four extracts which are all concerned in some way with music. For questions **19–26**, choose the answer (**A**, **B**, **C** or **D**) which you think fits best according to the text.

Choir practice

The sun is creeping over the Fenland horizon. As it does, so the Gothic spires of King's College, Cambridge, are tinted pink. In an upstairs room there is a horseshoe of high desks. At the focus of the horseshoe is a grand piano. Looking at the sheet music on the desks are 27 ordinary schoolboys aged between eight and thirteen dressed in white shirts, grey trousers and purple sweatshirts and ties. The height of the desks ensures that the boys sit up straight and take deep breaths. At the piano, Stephen Cleobury's gaze sweeps them through his spectacles, somewhere between amused and severe. 'One, two, three,' he says quietly, but with the rhythmic spring of a man already bearing music in his head. The boys begin to sing and things stop being ordinary.

The pitch is spot on. The tone is round and forceful enough to shake the windows. Away they go, with a sort of radiance that lights up the dreary morning, which is not surprising. For these are the 17 choirboys and ten probationers of King's College Chapel, whose next performance will be broadcast to millions of people worldwide. The first piece is practised, repractised and then left for another day. As the next sheets arrive on the desks, the boys run over it *sotto voce* before practising it. Hands are raised to acknowledge mistakes, which become fewer and further between as the practice progresses. Then it is 9.15 and the rehearsal is over. Out of the room they thunder into the ordinary world of school.

19 The furniture in the choir practice room
    A makes it easy for the boys to see the piano.
    B allows Stephen Cleobury to give instructions more effectively.
    C forces the boys to adopt the correct posture.
    D lets the boys focus more intensely.

20 What happens as the choir practice proceeds?
    A The boys make more mistakes.
    B It becomes obvious that the pieces are very difficult.
    C The choristers' singing improves.
    D The boys begin to feel tired.

A new force in music

Judging by the costly and chaotic attempts made by the music industry to suffocate file-sharing pioneers such as Napster, the moguls are refusing to come to terms with electronic distribution. Behind the scenes, however, times are changing. In public, pony-tailed bigwigs denounce the download revolution as online 'robbery' of artistic creativity, but in private, it has finally dawned on them that new technology cannot be ignored.

Now that this has been fully understood, the industry is belatedly fighting online for the loyalty of fans, but it may already be a lost cause. A second perhaps more serious threat has reared its head. Household names may soon come to realise that the net provides an escape route from the bondage of the record company.

The example of Marillion suggests a new business paradigm. Dropped by their record company, the band had to cancel a US tour until a fan, Jeff Woods, raised £37,000 online from other fans to fund the tour. Realising the potential of the net from this response, 13,000 fans each paid Marillion £16 in advance to allow the band to record *Anoraknophobia*. Suddenly, Marillion had their biggest recording advance and no record company to call the tune, proving that the net threatens the record industry, but frees the artist.

21 The writer describes file-sharers like Napster as
    A irresponsible.
    B innovative.
    C indiscriminate.
    D immoral.

22 Modern technology seems to have made the music business more
    A liberating for the performers.
    B suited to those with a lot of money.
    C difficult for performers not backed by a record company.
    D accessible to artists.

Miles Davis – *Kind of Blue*

When Miles Davis assembled a band for the sessions that would become *Kind of Blue*, he was already on his way to becoming a jazz legend. He had served an apprenticeship with bop icons, Charlie Parker and Dizzy Gillespie, come up with a whole new brand of accessible bebop-inspired music on his *Birth of the Cool* album and embarked on several big band experiments with arranger Gil Evans.

Before *Kind of Blue*, he was ready to change music again. He did it by going back to basics and by incorporating composer George Russell's theories on modal jazz – music based around particular scales (modes) rather than chord progressions or song structures. In this way he hoped to coerce his musicians into concentrating on melody, mood and tone and not to be restricted to playing standard changes.

It seems strange that the single most famous album in jazz, which more than any other typifies the small-hours mood of the jazz nightfly, was actually recorded during a couple of afternoons in March and April, 1959. The majority of it was conceived just a few hours before the first session, and none of the musicians had heard the themes before. Miles Davis was after total improvisation with a minimum amount of pre-planning and he got it.

23 Throughout his career, Miles Davis
   A only worked with top names.
   B did not feel restricted by tradition.
   C inspired musicians to join the jazz scene.
   D was strict with musicians in his band.

24 What characterises the album *Kind of Blue*?
   A repeated rhythms
   B freedom of expression
   C pre-arranged chord progressions
   D a lack of cohesion

Soundless music

A shiver of anticipation swept through the audience as they took their seats in Liverpool's Metropolitan Cathedral for what was to be a recital with a difference. The soloist was a young Russian pianist but her accompanists were two scientists who were playing a five-metre sewer pipe. The pipe was designed to produce a frequency of 17.5 hertz, which is just below the threshold for audibility. So, although the pipe would have been inaudible, the aim was to see whether the audience would somehow be able to sense it was playing.

The recital, billed as *Soundless Music*, was the dress rehearsal in an experiment designed to answer this question. The experiment was the brainchild of Sarah Angliss, a composer, electroacoustics engineer and pianist. She was prompted to undertake the project by the fact that numerous organs have been built over the past 300 years with pipes that pump out bass notes below 20 hertz. Initially, she had hoped that organ builders themselves would be able to shed light on why these pipes had been included but was disappointed by their lack of consensus.

The Liverpool audience fared a little better, making such comments as 'the inaudible notes produced a tingly feeling in the back of my neck' and 'it gave a sense of presence'. Although these remarks did not help Angliss a great deal, she realises the experiment is still in its infancy.

25 What happened when organ builders were asked about the construction of organs?
   A Their answers were food for thought for Angliss.
   B They were secretive about their trade.
   C They gave several different answers.
   D They made light of the questions.

26 Angliss's experiment
   A was inspired by organists.
   B has attracted interest worldwide.
   C has been described as controversial.
   D has only just begun.

Part 3

You are going to read an extract from a novel. Seven paragraphs have been removed from the extract. Choose from the paragraphs **A–H** the one which best fits each gap (**27–33**). There is one extra paragraph which you do not need to use.

'Any weekday I think, during opening hours. Major Knox is a most punctual man ... except Wednesday afternoons, that is. He always has Wednesday afternoons off – for his golf, you know.'

27

Lunchtime the following day: ideal, I judged, to find the administrative quarters of Barrowteign at their quietest. I followed the tour route as far as the backstairs, then headed up instead of down. The corridor on the second floor was silent, with no clack of typewriter or jingle of telephone, Knox's secretary had evidently gone to lunch and Knox himself I knew would be out for the rest of the day.

28

It was simple to reach out and remove it and I knew I was safe from detection if I returned it before the end of the day. Hadn't Knox said nobody ever went up to the attics? Yet my heart pounded as I walked along the corridor towards the door leading to them. Strangely, it wasn't the fear of the daylight robber which had gripped me, but fear that I was now so close to discovering The Postscript: I'd dreamed about it, debated it, run over in my mind only that morning on the bus all the permutations of what it might contain. The prospect of certainty was suddenly intimidating.

29

I crouched in front of it, as Ambrose must have done, and prized gingerly at the drawbridge. It stuck fast – I hesitated to wrench at it. Then, the answer appeared: a rusty spindle embedded in the wall of the castle porch. It turned, squeakily but effectively – the drawbridge jerked down on a string cable.

30

With the string gone, I could raise the portcullis by one finger lodged in the grille. I was on my knees now, peering in through the narrow gateway. Sure enough, by the dim light I could see, as I held up the portcullis, an object – stowed inside. I reached in with my other hand. It felt solid and book-shaped, the wrapper vaguely waxy, tied with rough string. I eased it out from its resting place. There was a struggle to get it past the spikes of the portcullis. Then it was free and in my hands.

31

It could have been the Memoir looking back at me: the same style of book – a leather-bound, maroon-covered tome with marbled pages, standard issue, perhaps in the Consular Service. Unlike the Memoir, most of its pages were blank, but the first quarter or so was filled with that distinctive, copperplate handwriting in diplomatic black ink that left no doubt in my mind. Strafford had left his mark. Just when I'd begun to fear I'd never hear his voice again, here he was, speaking to me only as he could.

32

I left the wrapping paper and string by the castle and walked over to one of the windows, a grimy fanlight admitting a sepia beam into the attic. Outside, there was a lead gully forming a gutter, a brick parapet beyond it and blue sky. The gully was broad and dry, the brightness inviting. The fanlight opened in the centre. I wrenched down the retaining bolts and pushed the two halves apart. They stuck for a moment, then swung free.

33

From the parapet, I had an imposing view of the garden. A few tiny figures were moving among the fountains and clipped hedges. Beyond them, the foothills of the Haldon range climbed eastwards. The scene shimmered in a modest heat haze. It could have been painted or embroidered – a pattern of English country life laid out like a rug. A scene four generations of Straffords could have looked at smugly, the greenery refulgent with their ownership. But not any more. The Straffords were dead, strangers were loose in their garden – one on the roof of their house.

A We passed through one panel doorway into the next part of the attic. As before, there was an excess of riches. Under every dustsheet, behind every box, could have been the answer. A battered and strapped old cricket bat was propped against a hamper in one corner. Had Strafford once hit the village bowling for six with it? No. It was a boy's bat. Perhaps he'd instructed Ambrose in its use, on his return from the Great War.

B It was a waxed canvas package, securely wrapped and tied. I cursed myself for not bringing a penknife and told myself to be patient as I coaxed the knot loose. At last, the string fell away. I folded back the canvas, then an inner layer of crinkled brown paper – and there it was.

C Inside, a matched grille representing a portcullis appeared. And, in the other wall of the porch there was another smaller spindle. But this one was broken. It hung slackly, the string having perished years before, or severed in Ambrose's haste to pull it.

D A rush of sunlight and birdsong pierced the attic. I put my hand out and looked along the gully in either direction. It was quite a heat trap behind its parapet and just the airy hideaway I was looking for. I dragged over an old ottoman and, using it as a platform, I climbed out of the window.

E I closed the attic door carefully behind me, locked it and climbed the stairs to the windowless ante-chamber. Then I entered the attic itself. Sunlight split the gloom in dust-hung wedges. I threaded my way anxiously through the hoard of rubbish. There, safe in its niche by the angle of a joint, was the toy castle.

F There was a sound somewhere in the attic. With a start, I snapped the book shut, sending up a cloud of dust. I coughed and cursed my nerves. It was just a mouse scurrying among the packing cases. The door, after all, was locked behind me. Nevertheless, I felt vulnerable in that labyrinth of dusty rafters. I needed air, light and time to study my discovery.

G 'Thanks, I'll remember that.' There was no danger I wouldn't. It was Tuesday afternoon. I had only to wait twenty-four hours and Knox would be absent from his post. The key and the attic would be at my disposal.

H I walked slowly to his office, trying not to creak too many floorboards. Sunlight was streaming through the window behind his desk. A snatch of childish laughter came from the garden below. There, on the board by the door, was key number twelve.

Part 4

You are going to read an extract from an article about early New York gangs. For questions **34-40**, choose the answer (**A, B, C,** or **D**) which you think fits best according to the text.

THE STORM BEFORE THE CALM

The image New York conjures up is usually one of bright lights and high-powered executives, but it has not always been the wonderful town of Frank Sinatra's popular song. Just as London had its violent, chaotic birth pangs, so New York was terrorised for the best part of a century by a succession of gangs that originated from the criminal breeding ground bordered by Broadway, Canal Street and the Bowery.

Wave after wave of immigrants from Ireland, Italy and Eastern Europe only served to sharpen the ferocity with which the indigenous New York gangs defended their turf. There were the Swamp Angels, who swarmed uptown in their droves through the city's sewers on their missions of mayhem. There were the Daybreak Boys, who specialised in recruiting cut-throats aged ten or eleven. There were the common-or-garden street toughs like Stumpy Malarkey and Googoo Knox who would team up with organisations like the infamous Dead Rabbit Gang. One of the Dead Rabbits, Hell-Cat Maggie, prepared for battle by filing her front teeth to points. Her comrade-in-arms, Sadie the Goat, butted her victims senseless before laying them out cold.

The violence on the streets simmered in an urban cauldron of soaring inflation, sweatshop squalor and working-class resentment until 1863, when Abraham Lincoln's National Conscription Act was passed. This was the spark that ignited all-out gang war against the state. The Act made all able-bodied men eligible for the draft, which meant they would have to go to war against the Confederate South. To the Irish, who could not afford the $300 that middle-class New Yorkers were permitted to pay to dodge the draft, it seemed that poor white working men were being forced to fight for the freedom of Southern blacks, who would then come up north and take their jobs. As a result of this reasoning, the enraged Irish, led by gangs such as the Dead Rabbits, set fire to federal property, attacked newspaper offices and directed their anger towards any blacks who crossed their path. These were the worst civil disturbances in American history and for a week in July 1863 it appeared as though the entire city would burn to the ground.

This strife threw up characters that would shape these troubled times. The ace intimidator, Piker Ryan, was one such individual. When he was finally arrested, a price list of intimidation was found in his pocket. It ranged from $2 for punching, $10 for a broken jaw and nose, through $15 for an ear chewed off to $100 and up for 'doing the big job'. Ryan was a member of the notorious Whyos, who were at the height of their power in the 1880s and 1890s. Other 'personalities' included Hoggy Walsh, Googy Corcoran and Baboon Connolly, all of whom were proficient in a wide variety of criminal activities.

And then there was Edward Delaney, a.k.a. Joseph Marvin and a number of other aliases. Delaney was the leader of a gang of 1,200 and quite unmistakable. He had a bullet-shaped head, a bull neck and heavily-scarred cheeks. During his career, he also acquired a broken nose, two cauliflower ears and a ferocious demeanour, which he accentuated with a derby hat several sizes too small, perched on top of his bristly, battered scalp.

By the end of the century, however, the pressure subsided due to a boom that had begun to make the city respectable at last. As the tide of violence receded, the gangs became more and more confined to the Five Points. Here, they would enjoy a glorious swansong before being swept up in the cosmic violence of the First World War. Between 1900 and 1914, the gangs rejected their coarse traditions and became shaved, manicured dandies. Johnny Spanish, for example, never left home without a lily of the field in his buttonhole and the much-feared bruiser, Biff Ellison, was a snappy dresser who loved to sprinkle himself with a scent specially prepared for him. These were the changes that marked the end of an era.

To historians, this period has several contemporary parallels. There will inevitably be conflict between newer waves of immigrants and the older assimilated groups. These reflect the struggle to be free for every cultural group when they find themselves in an environment where so many races, colours and creeds are thrown together in the proverbial melting pot.

34 What is implied as being the Swamp Angels' greatest asset during confrontations?
   A   the sheer size of the gang
   B   the fact that they didn't mind getting dirty
   C   their fearlessness
   D   their ferocity

35 Why was Sadie of the Dead Rabbits nicknamed 'the Goat'?
   A   She had sharp teeth.
   B   She lacked intelligence.
   C   She used her head as a weapon.
   D   She gave no thought to her victims.

36 Why did the Irish react so violently to the Conscription Act?
   A   They thought it would probably lead to their being unemployed.
   B   They resented the fact that only the Irish had to go to war.
   C   They felt they needed proper training before going to war.
   D   Their chances of surviving the war were slim.

37 The civil disturbances of 1863
   A   were aggravated by newspaper reports.
   B   claimed the lives of many major gangland figures.
   C   produced several infamous personalities.
   D   led directly to the downfall of many large gangs.

38 Why does the writer begin the fifth paragraph 'And then there was Edward Delaney...'?
   A   He was the last of the notorious gangsters.
   B   Nobody is quite sure what his real name was.
   C   He was the most fierce gangster.
   D   He was less important than other gang leaders.

39 Between 1900 and 1914
   A   top gang members tried to become more sophisticated.
   B   gangs began to take interest in musicals.
   C   tough gangsters went soft.
   D   many gang members decided they didn't want to be in a gang any more.

40 What is the conclusion reached in the final paragraph?
   A   New York's experiences are historically unique.
   B   A multicultural society can expect violent struggles.
   C   Social development can only occur through violent acts.
   D   New ideas result in cultural conflict.

Test Three

Paper 2: Writing

Part 1

You must answer this question. Write your answer in **300-350** words in an appropriate style.

1   You have read the extract below while on a college education course. You have been asked to write an essay on the topic, commenting on the points raised and adding your own views on the subject.

> Schoolchildren are expected to take so many subjects these days that they cannot possibly study anything in depth, leaving them with only superficial knowledge. Moreover, some of the traditional subjects on the curriculum have little relevance to the modern world and give students no idea of how to cope when they begin work.

Write your **essay**.

Part 2

Write an answer to one of the questions **2-4** in this part. Write your answer in **300-350** words in an appropriate style.

2   An ecology magazine has invited readers to contribute an article for a new section in the magazine called *How to Make a Difference*. Write an article describing ways in which ordinary people can help protect the environment.

   Write your **article**.

3   You have recently returned from a holiday in a foreign country. Write a letter to a travel magazine describing the effects of globalisation on the place you visited and how you feel about it.

   Write your **letter**.

4   You have recently seen a film with English subtitles at the cinema. Write a review of the film for a college magazine and say what effect watching the film with English subtitles had on you.

   Write your **review**.

Test Three

Hints on writing an article

An article is a piece of writing usually intended to be read in a magazine, newspaper, brochure or leaflet. Depending on who is going to read it, it can be formal or informal in style and could give information, advice, suggestions, a description of a place, event or experience or perhaps present a balanced argument or opinion.

An important part of an article (so that it actually looks like an article) is its headline or title. It should be eye-catching and should suggest what the article is about because in real life this is what helps you to decide whether to read an article or not. Remember to have a title at the beginning of your article as you will lose marks if you do not.

In the introduction, you should clearly state what you are going to write about. In the two to four paragraphs which follow, you must develop the subject in detail. Finally, the conclusion should summarise what you have written and include suggestions, comments or your opinion.

Before writing an article you need to think about where the article is going to appear and who the intended readers are. The purpose of the article is also important. Is it meant to offer advice or to provide information, for instance? Read the information carefully in the question as it will help you determine the style (formal or semi-formal), the type of language you will use, and the organisation of your article.

Depending on who its target readers are, an article can be written in an amusing or interesting style as it should give opinions and ideas as well as facts. A formal article, though, would include frequent use of the passive, sophisticated vocabulary, complex sentence structures, no contractions (*I'm*, *hasn't*, etc), no informal idioms and have formal connectors or phrases.

Make sure that you have had plenty of practice before attempting to write an article in an exam.

Test Three

Paper 3: Use of English

Hints on gap-filling sets of three sentences (Part 3)

In this part of the Use of English paper, there are six sets of three sentences with a gap in each one that you have to complete with a suitable word. The same word should fit all three sentences in each set.

For example:

Feel .... to help if you've got nothing to do.
We're thinking about seeing a film, and I was wondering if you're .... tonight.
Admission at weekends is .... to children under 10.

| FREE |

Always read all of the sentences before you answer. Make sure that you look at the words after the gap before you write anything, not just up to the gap. Often you will be able to find a word that fits the gap in one of the three sentences but make sure it definitely goes in the other two sentences as well. Prepositions after the gap are a helpful clue. You are being tested on collocations, phrasal verbs, idioms and lexical patterns.

Each sentence in isolation has more than one possible answer, but only one option will fit in all three sentences. The word will be the same part of speech and in the same form.

Once you have written your answer, read the whole sentence again to see that what you have written makes sense.

Use all the clues that are given to you and attempt to answer every question.

Test Three

Part 1

For questions **1-15**, read the text below and think of the word which best fits each space. Use only one word in each space. There is an example at the beginning (**0**).

Example: **0** ON

What's in a name

For most people, deciding (0) ......ON...... a name for a child is a relatively straightforward affair. For (1) .... there can be pitfalls. If you happen to have a common surname (2) .... Smith or Jones and are content to (3) .... from the list of traditional first names such as David, John and Susan, then the decision will be that much simpler.

Those who opt (4) .... a more unusual name may do so at their own peril. Should they approach the naming procedure too hastily, the child could (5) .... up with a name which will only bring a lifetime of resentment. (6) .... the footballer David Beckham, for example. Although his first child, Brooklyn, has an 'exotic' name, Brooklyn Beckham sounds fine. However, if his England team-mate Wayne Bridge (7) .... to do the same, his child would be named (8) .... a feat of engineering.

There are also some less obvious howlers than this. In these cases, it is not (9) .... the first name that has to be considered. For instance, a Mr and Mrs Day (10) .... name their daughter Denise or Dionne, but if people call her Dee, (11) .... is short for these names, she would become a moment in history. The same difficulties would apply (12) .... a Rosemary Bush, for instance.

Then there are those who deliberately (13) .... out to give their children such striking names that they are more (14) .... to be remembered. Or it might be that the person changes their name on their (15) .... for publicity purposes. Names in these two categories include Red Buttons, the actor, Muddy Waters, the musician, and Julia Caesar, a BBC presenter.

Part 2

For questions **16-25**, read the text below. Use the word given in capitals at the end of some of the lines to form a word that fits in the space in the same line. There is an example at the beginning (**0**).

Example: **0** SECOND

A literary giant

Born in Portsmouth, England, on 7th February 1812, Charles Dickens was the (0) ......SECOND...... **TWO**
of eight children. His father was a clerk who worked for the Navy Pay office until his
(16) .... for debt. Charles was very young at the time of his father's incarceration **PRISON**
and the resulting financial (17) .... forced him to seek work at the age of **HARD**
twelve. The (18) .... that Charles experienced together with the social **DEPRIVE**
(19) .... he observed affected him deeply and would influence his writing. **JUST**

Although Charles had little formal (20) .... , he managed to teach himself **SCHOOL**
shorthand. This enabled him to get a job as a (21) .... reporter at a newspaper. **PARLIAMENT**
He went on to publish work in magazines but it was not until he published *The Pickwick Papers* that he became really successful. Another of his most celebrated works, *A Tale of Two Cities*, was written twenty years after he had read a book about the French Revolution and
(22) .... knew that he had to write a novel set in the same period. **INSTINCT**

Dickens' health began to deteriorate in the 1860s and the fact that he had begun to do public
(23) .... only aggravated his condition. He died on 9th June 1870. By the time of **READ**
his death, he had written 15 (24) .... novels and countless other works. He was **SUBSTANCE**
(25) .... a great literary figure whose name will always be associated with a **DOUBT**
criticism of greed and the notion that good will be rewarded.

Paper 3: Use of English

Part 3

For questions **26-31**, think of one word only which can be used appropriately in all three sentences. Here is an example (**0**).

Example:

0 Things looked .... until the bank approved a loan to keep my business afloat.
Your failure to secure the contract will certainly mean a .... mark against your name.
I knew I'd offended him as he gave me a .... look as I turned to leave.

| 0 | BLACK |

26 Every morning, pigeons .... in the square hoping to be fed by tourists.
From what you have told me, I .... that you would prefer to live in the countryside.
The experience she will .... in her present job will qualify her for a far better post in the future.

| 26 | |

27 Most of the offices in this building .... the harbour.
Make sure you do not .... any important people when you compile the guest list.
Jack's manager informed him that she'd .... his late arrival this time, but it would be recorded in future.

| 27 | |

28 Some university courses .... to be much more difficult than expected.
Having won several gold medals, the athlete felt he no longer had to .... himself to anyone.
The easiest way to .... your innocence is to establish a watertight alibi.

| 28 | |

29 It is alleged that the captain was by no means .... awake when the ship struck an iceberg.
It can be a great educational experience to travel far and ....
His original estimate of the cost of the repairs was well .... of the mark: the actual cost was twice as much.

| 29 | |

30 As there was one .... missing, the set of encyclopedias was incomplete.
The sheer .... of work some people take on leads to a great deal of stress.
Before remote controls, you had to walk to the TV to increase the ....

| 30 | |

31 Although her students saw the funny side of their teacher's story, the accident was no laughing ....
We'd been trying to solve the problem all afternoon, but Sylvia managed to find a solution within a .... of minutes.
Everyone looked upset, but nobody would tell me what the .... was.

| 31 | |

Test Three

Part 4

For questions **32-39**, complete the second sentence so that it has a similar meaning to the first sentence, using the word given. **Do not change the word given**. You must use between **three** and **eight** words, including the word given. Here is an example (**0**).

Example:

0 Don't pay any attention to what he says.
   pinch
   I'd take .... if I were you.

   | what he says with a pinch of salt |

32 If the venture is not meticulously planned, we will not go ahead with it.
   get
   Without meticulous .... the ground.

33 Brian and Mina refuse to talk to each other because they can't agree on a divorce settlement.
   terms
   Brian and Mina .... since their failure to agree on a divorce settlement.

34 On discovering the truth about the burglary, Minnie became extremely angry.
   rage
   Minnie flew .... out the truth about the burglary.

35 The footballer won't be transferred unless he passes a medical examination at his new club.
   subject
   The footballer's .... passing a medical examination at his new club.

36 By the time Mrs White realised her daughter was lying, it was too late.
   see
   Mrs White .... lies until it was too late.

37 You could have heard a pin drop after the manager said the factory would be closing.
   absolute
   There .... the workers that the factory would be closing.

38 The only thing Pauline has in common with her two sisters is her blue eyes.
   bears
   Apart from her blue eyes, Pauline .... her two sisters.

39 There's no way Margaret would ever call you a liar.
   accuse
   Margaret would .... lies.

71

Test Three

Paper 3: Use of English

Part 5

For questions **40-44**, read the following texts on dangerous Australian animals. For questions **40-43**, answer with a word or short phrase. You do not need to write complete sentences. For question **44**, write a summary according to the instructions given.

The undisputed ruler of the Australian coastal waters is the great white shark, whose fearsome reputation is legendary among those who have observed it in the flesh and those who have seen its huge, gaping, tooth-studded jaws in documentaries. Because of the fascination it commands, it has become a headline-grabber whenever its encounters have involved humans.

5 As in all areas of life, a massive presence is always regarded as impressive, but it is by no means the only characteristic worthy of attention. This applies equally to Australian marine life in the shape of the largely-unknown cone snail, a gastropod whose size is inversely proportional to the danger it poses. This mollusc may be dwarfed by its illustrious neighbour but it is just as effective at snaring its prey.

The cone snail buries itself in the sea bed, leaving only a 'siphon', which resembles a worm, exposed
10 to view. This appendage serves three functions: to allow the creature to breathe while hidden, to detect fish swimming nearby and to act as a lure for its prey. As soon as the fish gets within range, it releases a harpoon-like tooth into the victim, injecting it with a lethal cocktail of poisons on contact. This paralyses the fish immediately and begins the digestive process, allowing the cone snail to digest it at leisure.

40 Which two words in the first paragraph reinforce the idea that the great white shark's reputation is widespread?
....

41 What exactly does the word 'This' (line 6) refer to?
....

Mention the words 'dangerous snake' and most people will probably conjure up images of giant constrictors like the wide-girthed anaconda, or the seriously-poisonous king cobra. Few people's idea of extreme danger embodied in a snake would be the innocuous-looking coastal taipan. Yet this snake incontrovertibly belies its rather benign appearance with its highly-effective venom apparatus (it has the longest fangs of any Australian snake), venom toxicity, venom yield, strength, agility and aggression.

The coastal taipan's back, upper sides and tail may be yellowish, reddish-brown, dark brown or blackish-brown. Its large, long head is quite distinct from its slender neck and its eyes are relatively large, making it look rather appealing. It is rarely seen in the wild, preferring to take shelter in abandoned animal burrows in order to avoid confrontation. However, when it is cornered, it holds its body coils in loose, open loops with the neck raised slightly, ready to deliver one or more 'jab-bites' as soon as the intruder gets too close. Its reputation among herpetologists for accuracy and speed is well deserved.

When the taipan leaves its refuge due to hunger, it becomes a stealthy hunter of rodents and small birds. Like all snakes, it senses its prey with its flickering tongue. On reaching its prey, the taipan strikes, injecting venom during an open-mouthed jab-bite. The ungripped prey is allowed to pull away and attempt to escape so that the snake avoids injury from the rodent's teeth or the bird's beak. After a short delay, the taipan follows the scent of the injected poison and swallows its prey, which has succumbed to the venom. By the time the prey disappears, the poison has already begun the process of digestion.

42 Which three words support the claim that the taipan does not resemble a highly-dangerous snake.

....

43 Explain in your own words what is meant by the phrase 'avoid confrontation' in line 9.

....

44 In a paragraph of between **50 and 70** words, summarise **in your own words as far as possible**, the similarities and differences between the ways in which the cone snail and the coastal taipan catch their prey.

....
....
....
....
....
....
....
....

Test Three — Paper 4: Listening

Hints on answering the multiple-choice sections (Parts 1 and 3)

This is the most familiar task type and is used in Parts 1 and 3 of the exam. It is often used to test understanding of the attitudes and opinions of speakers, both stated and implied, as well as the ability to distinguish what was said from what was not said.

Multiple-choice exercises require you to understand the main points of the information. This does not necessarily mean that you must understand every word that you hear. The more you listen to English outside the classroom, such as the radio or television, the more it will help you with this part of the test as the speaker(s) will be speaking at native-speaker speed, using native-speaker stress, intonation, idioms and colloquialisms.

Read the questions through before you listen to the tape. This will help you to predict what you will hear and to know what you are listening for. This mirrors what happens in real-life situations when we all bring a variety of extra areas of knowledge to what we hear, such as knowledge of the context, the speaker and/or the subject. Answer as many questions as you can the first time you listen. Check your answers and complete anything you missed when you listen to the cassette for the second time. Do not panic if you miss an answer or lose your place, as the questions are in the same order as what you are listening to on the tape. There will probably be a couple of words that you do not know but you should still be able to guess their meaning from the context and find the correct answer.

Read each of the choices (A, B or C) or (A, B, C or D) carefully. If it states on the cassette, for example, that *some* people do something, then a distractor that has *many* people cannot be right. Try not to rush because you think you will miss the information for the next question.

When you transfer your answers to the answer sheet at the end, make sure you mark the correct letters for each question.

As with all multiple-choice tasks, do not leave a question unanswered. If you really do not know the answer, guess. You have at least a 25% or 33% chance of choosing the right answer.

Test Three

Part 1

You will hear four different extracts. For questions **1-8**, choose the answer (**A**, **B**, or **C**) which fits best according to what you hear. There are two questions for each extract.

Extract One

You hear a woman talking about her house.

1   Why was the woman initially unsure about having the interior of her home re-designed?
    A   She thought the designer's ideas might not work.
    B   She thought it would cost a lot of money.
    C   She didn't want to be on TV.

2   What is the woman's opinion of what has been done to her home?
    A   She is surprised at how different it is.
    B   She thinks the bamboo window blind is the best thing of all.
    C   She is extremely pleased.

Extract Two

You hear a man talking about exercise.

3   When the man had his heart attack
    A   he continued the way of life he had before.
    B   he changed to an office job.
    C   he took it seriously.

4   What does the man think about going out walking some days?
    A   It's very convenient.
    B   Sometimes he doesn't feel like going, but it's worth it.
    C   It's a form of exercise that doesn't cost anything.

Extract Three

You hear a female reporter outside the home of a celebrity couple.

5   What has not yet been confirmed?
    A   whether Cindy has left the flat
    B   whether the couple have been together for six years
    C   whether the luxury flat is now for sale

6   Over the last six months
    A   the couple's relationship has been casual.
    B   Rod has been seeing other women.
    C   the couple have had a series of fights.

Extract Four

You hear a man talking about bats.

7   What does the speaker think of the fact that it's illegal to disturb bats?
    A   He disapproves of it.
    B   He agrees with it.
    C   He has reservations about it.

8   What would be the speaker's advice to someone with a fear of bats?
    A   not to worry at all
    B   to be careful when there are bats around
    C   to beware of bats that pounce

Test Three

Paper 4: Listening

Part 2

You will hear a radio report about the Northern Lights. For questions **9-17**, complete the sentences with a word or short phrase.

The modern development of [___9___] has enabled us to understand the Northern Lights.

The auroral sub-storm involves the formation of [___10___] of light spreading all over the sky.

The speaker compares the rays during an auroral sub-storm to moving [___11___].

The sight of faint [___12___] or clouds of light signals the end of the Northern Lights activity.

At one time, the Northern Lights were used as the basis for forecasting the [___13___].

At the turn of the 20th century, it was believed the Northern Lights were caused by [___14___], in a similar way to thunder.

There seems to be a link between [___15___] weather and the Northern Lights.

The colder weather in the eighteenth century was called the Scandinavian [___16___].

Most people find it difficult to understand the [___17___] of the Northern Lights.

Part 3

You will hear an interview with Peter Robinson, a war reporter. For questions **18-22**, choose the answer (**A**, **B**, **C** or **D**) which fits best according to what you hear.

18 The speaker's desire for adventure
   - A helped to keep him alive.
   - B was part of his reason for becoming a war reporter.
   - C almost killed him.
   - D prompted him to find out about Indochina.

19 Why did the speaker say he went to Vietnam in 1970?
   - A His options were limited.
   - B His army unit was sent there.
   - C He was well-qualified for the job.
   - D The war had just started.

20 How did he feel on his first assignment?
   - A confident and calm
   - B irresponsible
   - C afraid and confused
   - D in charge of the situation

21 The speaker believed the young soldiers
   - A were fighting for a just cause.
   - B would probably die in Vietnam.
   - C should have been having fun instead.
   - D were having the time of their lives.

22 Why does the speaker relate the helicopter story?
   - A to demonstrate that there's humour in everything
   - B to show how dangerous helicopter travel can be
   - C to indicate how ill he'd been
   - D to prove how dreadful the war had been

Part 4

You will hear two people, Elaine and Frank, talking about writing a rock opera. For questions **23-28**, decide whether the opinions are expressed by only one of the speakers, or whether the speakers agree.

Write **E**   for Elaine
      F   for Frank
or   **B**   for Both, where they agree.

23 Several major rock operas made a huge impression on me.

24 Everyone can enjoy music.

25 It took a great deal of effort and disagreement to produce the first opera.

26 I was amazed when I saw how the rock opera was developing.

27 The key is in adapting the story and developing ideas from it.

28 It would be a good idea to adapt a different kind of story next time.

Test Three
Paper 5: Speaking

Part 1

- How long have you been studying English?
- How do you intend to use your English in the future?
- Why do you think it is important for people to be able to speak foreign languages?
- What other languages do members of your family speak?
- Would you like to live in England? Why, or why not?
- What places or countries have you visited in the past?
- Which country would you most like to visit? Why?

Part 2

Here are some pictures depicting different forms of the media. (Page 172)

a First I'd like you to look at pictures A and B and talk together about what kinds of information and entertainment we can obtain from each of the types of media displayed. You have about a minute for this.

b Now I'd like you to look at all the pictures. I'd like you to imagine that you could only have access to one of these forms of media.

Talk together about the merits of each medium, and then decide which you would choose in preference to all the others. You have three minutes to talk about this.

Part 3

In this part of the test you are going to talk on your own for about two minutes. You need to listen while your partner is speaking because you'll be asked to comment afterwards.

I'm going to give you a card with a question on it and I'd like you to say what you think. There are some ideas on the card for you to use if you like.

Candidate A, here is your card.

Prompt Card A

> How are people using the Internet these days?
> - buying products
> - news
> - communication

Candidate B, what do you think? (1 minute)
Candidates A and B, is the increase in Internet usage a good thing? (1 minute)

Candidate B, look at your card and say what you think. There are some ideas on the card for you to use if you like.

Prompt Card B

> What do you think are the most important recent advances in technology?
> - mobile phones
> - digital photography
> - surgery assisted by computer

Candidate A, how does this differ from your opinion? (1 minute)
Candidates A and B, what are the disadvantages of mobile phones? (1 minute)

Both candidates: Now to finish the test, we're going to talk about technology. (4 minutes)

- What are the implications of people increasingly using e-mails to communicate, rather than the telephone or letters?
- How important are computers in modern-day society?
- Are there any disadvantages to the huge advances in technology that have recently been made?
- Are there areas where you think modern technology is currently under-utilised?

Test Three

Hints on discussing pictures

After the personal questions that the interviewer will ask you, he/she will give you some photographs in **Part 2** which you will have to discuss within a certain context, and this may involve some comparing and contrasting of the pictures. The interviewer will assess how you use vocabulary and how well you organise your language and ideas. Don't forget that in this part of the interview, you are expected to hold a discussion with the other candidate, so use phrases such as, *I agree, but don't you think that...* or *Sorry, but I think that...* . Remember that even if you do agree with what the other candidate is saying, sometimes it is easier to disagree, as you can add more to the conversation. Learn to disagree politely.

When you talk about the pictures, you may have to guess or deduce what the situation is. Modal verbs and words like *perhaps* or *maybe* are necessary but you need to vary your vocabulary more than that and not limit yourself. Use expressions such as:

> I imagine...
> I get the impression that...
> As far as I can tell, ...
> I should think...
> My impression is...
> I suppose...
> In my opinion, ...
> It looks (to me) as if/though...

Here are some other useful expressions:

> - He might/may be + -ing / Maybe he is + -ing
> - She could be + -ing
> - They might have been + -ing
> - They could have been + -ing (referring to completed actions)

Also remember to use the second conditional when appropriate.

For example: *If I had more time, I would choose...*

Using a variety of structures and expressions shows your command of the language.

You will not have to describe a photograph in much detail but remember to use the present continuous as the activity in the picture is still happening.

Paper 1: Reading

Hints on one text with multiple choice (Part 4)

This is one text followed by seven four-option multiple choice questions.

Because the text in this part is quite long, it's important to have a basic grasp of the arguments and ideas in it before attempting the questions.

You are bound to be faced with a lot of unfamiliar vocabulary in Part 4 of the Reading Paper. Remember that the context can give you a fairly good idea of what they mean, and it is very rare that the correct answer to a question will depend on the meaning of a single word.

Very often the three distractors will partly paraphrase ideas in the text using synonyms of words and phrases that appear in the text. Consequently, a distractor might at first glance seem to be correct. Make sure that your choice is an accurate paraphrase and that it actually answers the question.

Due to the length of the text in this part, time management is very important. You will need to be able to tell what information is irrelevant to the questions. You can save time, then, by reading the questions before beginning the text.

Although the questions in this part will always follow the order of the passage, information in the distractors may still be found throughout the text. The last question often tests you on your general understanding of the text.

Test Four

Part 1

For questions 1-18, read the three texts below and decide which answer (**A, B, C,** or **D**) best fits each gap.

QUICKSAND

Well aware of the danger posed by quicksand, country dwellers wisely (1) .... clear of it and stay out of trouble. Those, on the other hand, who are (2) .... with its properties may not always give it the wide berth it demands. When this happens, the intruder is literally (3) .... with death for quicksand can and very often does prove lethal.

Quicksand is formed by a (4) .... called liquefaction, which occurs when water mixes with sand. The resulting mixture is very dangerous because the more a trapped person or animal struggles, the further into it they sink. In the end, the victim gets well and (5) .... stuck, with little hope of escape. Normally, there are only isolated examples of people (6) .... prey to the sludge, but in 1679 a whole town in Jamaica sank in quicksand, resulting in the death of 200 people.

1	A	steer	B	navigate	C	tread	D	get
2	A	unfamiliar	B	unknown	C	uncommon	D	unaccustomed
3	A	dabbling	B	toying	C	risking	D	dicing
4	A	routine	B	process	C	technique	D	procedure
5	A	properly	B	undeniably	C	invariably	D	truly
6	A	becoming	B	resulting	C	falling	D	ending

FOOTBALL HOOLIGAN TO OPERA SINGER

As a teenager, Mark Glanville went to a tough state secondary school where he felt like a (7) .... out of water. Feeling a natural need to belong, he took up judo and became a 'Cockney Red', the term used to describe London's Manchester United supporters. On the football terraces, he (8) .... a taste for violence as a channel for his volcanic anger. Despite his excessive teenage confusion, he managed to get into Oxford University and, in order not to (9) .... himself from his hooligan pals, he explained his absence by saying that he had been sent to prison. While he was 'in jail', he substituted football hooliganism for breaking into wine cellars with a more sophisticated gang. As well as breaking the law, Mark discovered he had a talent for singing and (10) .... at the Royal Northern College of Music after leaving Oxford.

When his singing career finally (11) .... , he put his wild past behind him and got married. This was the final episode in the remarkable transformation of a thug intent on (12) .... violence to a purveyor of culture.

7	A	shark	B	fish	C	dolphin	D	crab
8	A	adapted	B	assumed	C	adopted	D	acquired
9	A	alienate	B	estrange	C	detach	D	expunge
10	A	enrolled	B	joined	C	enlisted	D	entered
11	A	went up	B	got up	C	took off	D	carried away
12	A	invoking	B	inciting	C	coercing	D	coaxing

A MAYAN HISTORY LESSON

The latest in a (13) .... line of theories to account for the disappearance of the Mayan empire has been put forward. This scientific theory lays the blame for the demise of this revered civilisation (14) .... on the shoulders of a 200-year drought in Central America. The Mayans, whose empire reached its (15) .... around 700 AD, were simply unable to grow crops without water and starved to death.

Although this theory sounds perfectly plausible, to historians it is flawed since they generally believe that only changes such as war, trade or rebellion can affect the (16) .... of history. Nevertheless, these findings have (17) .... implications for the future of humanity. This is because the present situation of (18) .... global water supplies may be further exacerbated by global warming, which would ultimately make humankind vulnerable to climatic disruption.

13	A	far	B	long	C	extensive	D	distant
14	A	squarely	B	forcefully	C	totally	D	heavily
15	A	apex	B	crest	C	summit	D	peak
16	A	course	B	path	C	route	D	way
17	A	consequential	B	heavy	C	profound	D	expansive
18	A	reducing	B	diminishing	C	eroding	D	deteriorating

81

Paper 1: Reading

Part 2

You are going to read four extracts which are all concerned in some way with property. For questions **19-26**, choose the answer (**A, B, C** or **D**) which you think fits best according to the text.

Superstitions

In these days of diminishing opportunities, you would not think that people could be put off moving into 13 Briars Road or 666 Laurel Avenue. Many first-time buyers, you might assume, would consider it a lucky omen to be able to get a foot on the first rung of the property ladder. But with a reported one in ten people afflicted by triskaidekaphobia (the fear of the number 13), it seems that there is more than bricks and mortar in play when it comes to moving house.

One solution to this fear is to request a change in house number to the less scary 12A, but more drastic action has been taken. An elderly lady selling a period house had an actual dagger embedded underneath the front step. It was there to ward off evil spirits and she was adamant that it should remain there after the property had been sold. And it is not only the number 13 that is feared. Chinese buyers, for instance, avoid houses numbered four, which sounds like a word for death in Cantonese and Mandarin. Small wonder, then, that in a new block in Hampstead, London, the apartments on the upper floors are numbered 10, 11, 12, 15 and 16 in order to ensure that no prospective buyers are deterred by a number.

19 Why does the writer think it's surprising that first-time buyers might refuse a house because of its number?
  A He considers it lucky.
  B He thinks they are being ridiculous.
  C There are fewer and fewer chances to find houses these days.
  D They are very well built.

20 One elderly seller of a house
  A buried a good luck charm near its entrance.
  B refused to change its number.
  C would not leave after it had been sold.
  D changed the number to 12A.

A LASTING INFLUENCE

From the outside, Heatherage Barn, deep in rural Lancashire looks like a standard conversion. Step inside, though, and you enter a remarkable interior which pays homage to the designs of Charles Rennie Mackintosh. Mackintosh was an architect and artist known for his innovative blend of art nouveau and Scottish influences. Born in 1868, he designed the Glasgow School of Art in his home town, where he received far less recognition than he did in Europe. He died in obscurity in 1928.

The brick barn in the village of Woodplumpton, near Preston, has been restored in Mackintosh's elegant geometric style, partly developed from Japanese influences after he broke with art nouveau. The fact that the owner has been influenced by Mackintosh's style is evident in the crisp hallmarks of dark furnishings set against white walls and objects with his distinctive violet and silver note. Natural light floods some areas, while electric light bulbs cast deep shadows in others.

The converted barn owners' passion for Mackintosh is a small part of the increasing popularity of his unique style. Those who have joined his growing army of admirers are astonished by the fact that although the designs were created during and shortly after the Victorian era, they seem so sleek and contemporary.

21 At the time of his death, Charles Rennie Mackintosh
  A had been completely forgotten.
  B was in the middle of a change of style.
  C was principally concerned with renovations.
  D lectured at the Glasgow School of Art.

22 Mackintosh's designs are characterised as being
  A popular in Victorian Scotland.
  B rather eccentric.
  C ahead of their time.
  D influenced by his contemporaries.

Making space

After the loft has been converted and an extension built, there should be enough room in the house. But what if it is still too small and expanding upwards or outwards is impractical or impossible? The answer may very well lie beneath as converting dank cellars into pleasant, dry living areas is becoming increasingly popular. An existing cellar can be tanked (given a waterproof lining), plastered, decorated and given a new staircase at a relatively low cost. This can be reasonably estimated as being on a par with that of a simple conversion.

Unfortunately, in Britain cellars are not standard as they are in the US or Germany. At best, there is very often only an old-fashioned coal cellar running underneath the front hall. Although it will cost more, these can be dug out to give proper head height and become usable. The added expense will come not only from the digging but from the underpinning that will probably be needed. All this may sound daunting, but an extra storey could effectively be added without any obvious change to outward appearance. This could add a significant amount to the market value and provide a soundproof room where children or teenagers can play as noisily as they wish without disturbing the peace.

23 Converting a standard cellar into living space
 A is less of a practical solution in Britain than in other countries.
 B requires extensive work to the exterior of the house.
 C cannot be carried out before a loft conversion.
 D is most easily accomplished in old houses.

24 The extra work required to convert a coal cellar into another room
 A is not as big a job as it seems.
 B is not compensated for by the increase in market value.
 C won't always guarantee a room of adequate height.
 D should not require much time to complete.

THE TRICKS OF THE TRADE

The game's up. It has been given away by an attractive vase of flowers and the guilty party is the estate agent. The vase of flowers in question appeared in a glossy brochure produced for clients who wanted to sell their house at the best price they could get for it. The flowers, brilliant white and beautifully arranged, were lending a touch of class to the property. They looked splendid on the kitchen table. Yet by an extraordinary coincidence, an identical vase of flowers appeared on the dining table and in the sitting room. There also seemed to be a bottle of champagne and a couple of glasses doing the rounds.

Producing property brochures for potential buyers is an exact science. Needless to say, the most important element is the photographs. There should probably be a maximum of five. Before photographing begins, the first thing that any self-respecting expert in this field will do is clear away any clutter, starting with the mantelpiece. They will also make sure there is a fire burning cosily in the grate and that the indoor lights are on, regardless of the time of year or day.

In the world of the glossy brochure, the flattering angle will always be found. And if a house is just too ugly, there will be a shot from the terrace showing a view across the water. The tricks of the trade have been revealed and the cat is well and truly out of the bag.

25 The first step taken before photographing a house for a property brochure is
 A to choose the right flower arrangement to use.
 B to find out what prospective clients like.
 C to remove all unwanted objects from view.
 D to check the lighting inside the house.

26 How do brochures compensate for imperfections inside the house?
 A They include several photos of the same room taken from different angles.
 B Photographs of the exterior are featured more prominently.
 C There are fewer photographs and more descriptions.
 D They will include pictures of other, more attractive properties.

Paper 1: Reading

Part 3

You are going to read an article about verbal skills. Seven paragraphs have been removed from the article. Choose from the paragraphs **A–H** the one which best fits each gap (27–33). There is one extra paragraph which you do not need to use.

It began with grunts and very soon it may end with them. Excess hours in front of the television together with parents who work long hours are robbing our children of humanity's most precious evolutionary attribute: language – 'the dress of thought', as Samuel Johnson described our capacity for intelligent speech.

27

In other words, we face a world in which intelligible communication is likely to become a rarity. A logical conclusion, perhaps, but it must be borne in mind that the death of language has been predicted many times in the past by such respected figures as George Bernard Shaw. Nevertheless, most parents would find it hard not to agree with Wells's basic message.

28

It is a worrying trend, not just for those who lose an ability to use language, he says, but for the fate of the planet as a whole. Robbed of an ability to follow and sustain complex arguments, more and more humans will simply give up trying to understand or influence the world around them, including the key international challenges we face like global warming and cloning.

29

Indeed, it is a particularly alarming prospect for a species that is distinguished by its communication skills. Language has been found in every one of the thousands of societies documented by scientists and is used by every neurologically normal member of humanity. As Steve Parker, director of the Centre of Cognitive Neuroscience at Massachusetts Institute of Technology, says: 'Language is so tightly woven into human experiences that it is scarcely possible to imagine life without it.'

30

The observation suggests that the root of human language is social, not intellectual, and that its usefulness in communicating complex notions came relatively late in our evolutionary history. For most of our time on Earth, language has had the equivalent role of grooming among monkeys, strengthening social bonds between individuals and cementing tribes together.

31

Only relatively late in the story of Homo Sapiens has language emerged in its current mature version. Recent work by Simon Fisher at the Welcome Trust Centre for Human Genetics in Oxford and Svante Paabo, at the Max Planck Institute of Evolutionary Anthropology in Leipzig, Germany, has dated key mutations in genes involved in neurone activity to about 200,000 years ago. These, they say, may have been crucial to our acquisition of sophisticated speech.

32

It is precisely at this time, of course, that modern Homo Sapiens evolved in an area of sub-Saharan Africa. Armed with a new linguistic sophistication, they poured out of Africa and by 40,000 years ago had reached the edge of Europe, then the stronghold of massive, cold-adapted Neanderthals, who nevertheless succumbed to these African interlopers, even though the continent was then in the grip of the last Ice Age. Above all, it was our ability to exchange complex data that gave us an advantage in those harsh days.

33

In short, language has been a mixed blessing for humanity. But it is what defines us as a species and it is hard to imagine us losing our prowess in the long term. 'In any case, just because our kids grunt at us, it doesn't mean to say they cannot communicate,' says Dunbar. 'It probably just means they don't want to talk to adults.'

A   It is a worrying vision, summed up by one senior education expert – Alan Wells, director of the government's Basic Skills Agency – who warned that youngsters now communicate in monosyllables, mainly because parents have lost the art of talking and playing with their children. 'At the age when they come into school, many children have very few language skills at all and that clearly has an impact on their learning,' he told an education conference.

B   'I have got to admit that I feel more than a twinge of sympathy,' said linguistic expert, Professor Robin Dunbar of Liverpool University. 'Judging from my own kitchen table, intelligent speech does sometimes seem to be at a premium among youngsters these days.'

C   Intriguingly, recent research suggests that language may have developed in combination with the use of music and singing. 'Our work suggests early humans engaged in a lot of chanting and choral singing,' he says. 'It is the equivalent of tribal singing on football terraces or Welsh community singing – that sort of thing. It was a way of identifying ourselves.'

D   As well-meaning parents, we try to compensate for this lack of communication. Every now and then, we attempt to engage our children in friendly dialogue, only to be met with baleful stares or goggle-eyed incomprehension, and something along the lines of 'er, neugh, ugh.'

E   After that, humanity slowly conquered all the nooks and crannies of the planet, from the tip of South America to the islands of Polynesia. To every one of these outposts, we brought language. Then around 10,000 years ago, agriculture was invented and in its wake the ability to write down words, which were needed to record the corn, wheat and oxen we began to trade in. At the same time, social ranks, possessions and war also appeared. As Aldous Huxley said: 'Thanks to words, we have been able to rise above the brutes – and thanks to words, we have often sunk to the level of the demons.'

F   'Essentially, more and more people will give up thinking and following these issues and leave them in the hands of eloquent experts, who will take on the roles of shamans. That is hardly a healthy development,' said Dunbar.

G   'We have studied a gene called FOXP2, which is known to have a role in brain development,' says Fisher. 'It is found in mammals from mice to chimpanzees with hardly any variation between any two species except for humans. Our version has several key alterations and, by studying their frequency among different tribes, we have shown that these mutations appeared about 200,000 years ago. Most probably, these changes would have enhanced early humans' ability to control the muscles of their mouth and face, crucial in the development of speech.'

H   The importance of speech in our lives is revealed by the fact that a person may utter as many as 40,000 words in a day. However, the intriguing point, as uncovered by Dunbar, is that most of these are about trivial issues. By monitoring common-room chat, Dunbar discovered that 86 per cent of our daily conversations are about personal relationships and experiences, TV programmes and jokes. We may be able to outline the theory of relativity or the ideas of Freud, but we rarely bother to do so. Most of the time, we use language to gossip. 'It is what makes the world go round,' Dunbar says.

Paper 1: Reading

Part 4

You are going to read an article about Neanderthals and Cro-Magnons. For questions **34-40**, choose the answer (**A**, **B**, **C**, or **D**) which you think fits best according to the text.

THE EARLY DAYS

In their heyday, between 127,000 and 40,000 years ago, Neanderthals were quite successful, spreading out from Europe to populate the Middle East and south-west Asia. But then the first European representatives of modern humans, popularly known as Cro-Magnons, began to appear. Two factors may account for the triumph of our ancestors.

First they had developed a new tool kit that included various side scrapers, the burin (a chisel-like tool), and the awl, all made by modifying long thin flakes, or blades, of stone that had been struck off a prepared core. With this lithic tool kit, the Cro-Magnons were able to manufacture points for hunting from materials such as antler, bone and ivory and, by doing so, turned the animals' own weapons, their horns and tusks, against them. Nevertheless, some Neanderthals – those who survived in relatively dense populations in close proximity to Cro-Magnons – were also able to make use of the new technology.

The second reason for the success of the Cro-Magnons was, paradoxically, the increasingly inhospitable climate. Although the most bitter glacial conditions had not descended on Europe 40,000 years ago, the centre and the north of the continent were cold. The irony here is that Neanderthals were biologically better adapted to the cold than Cro-Magnons were. But through language and other symbolic systems, the Cro-Magnons were able to make more effective cultural and ecological adaptations to the climate, and to form alliances among groups separated by great distances.

Those accomplishments of modern humans may have arisen through the sharing of stories and old myths that linked people with the natural world and with their common ancestors. Modern humans were also proud wearers of personal ornaments, whose use probably supported group organisation and identification. As worsening environmental conditions reduced the human population in number and density, symbolic communication took on even greater significance. Finally, even the stable Mediterranean world was dramatically affected by climate change. Forests gave way to steppes and large herds of horses, soon to be followed by horse hunters.

The difference in the ways Neanderthals and Cro-Magnons confronted the hostile climate is abundantly clear if one looks east to the Russian Plain. This vast, low-lying plain stretches from the Carpathian Mountains in the west to the Ural Mountains in the east and to the Arctic Ocean in the north. In the south, it ends at the Black Sea, the Caspian Sea, and the solid wall of the Caucasus Mountains which lies between the two. In the present warm period of the twenty-first century, the average January temperature at the centre of the area, at 50 degrees north latitude, is -24°C. It is by no means a hospitable place to spend a night in the open.

The first humans who dared to migrate into the Russian Plain were Neanderthals. The migration began about 120,000 years ago in the interglacial period that preceded the last glaciation. They reached sites as far as 52 degrees north latitude. There is no doubt, then, that they were able to adapt to extreme conditions, and it is hard to deny that they must have possessed an extraordinary aptitude for organisation and planning. Despite their adaptability, the Neanderthals were forced to retreat south when the last glaciation arrived. They took refuge on the Crimean Peninsula and the northern slopes of the Caucasus Mountains. The last of them probably disappeared from the area between 25,000 and 30,000 years ago.

The Cro-Magnons, in contrast, succeeded in conquering the Russian Plain, apparently using bone awls and needles to make garments as warm as the ones worn by the modern Inuit. As the last ice age reached a ferocious climax, the Cro-Magnons learned to build shelters framed with mammoth bones and covered with skins, and to keep their hearths burning within the shelters. When other fuels were scarce, they fed the fire with mammoth bones.

Meanwhile, 32,000 years ago, modern people had occupied almost the entire European Continent. Spectacular examples of their symbolic expression are preserved in Paleolithic art, from painted friezes in Chauvet Cave in south eastern France to animal statuettes of ivory in Vogelherd Cave in Germany. By this time, the Neanderthals had lost a lot of their former territory, though they still occupied the whole of the Iberian Peninsula, except for a band across the far north. The geographical boundary between Cro-Magnons and Neanderthals in northern Iberia has been called the Ebro Frontier after the Ebro River. In general terms, the boundary also separates two large biogeographical regions: the green 'Euro-Siberian' part of northern Iberia and the drier Mediterranean Iberia. According to archaeologists, this division is no coincidence. The Cro-Magnons came to Iberia from the Northern ecosystems of the Euro-Siberian world which contained misty forests filled with red deer, roe deer and boar as well as steppes with great herds of horses, reindeer, mammoths, woolly rhinoceroses, saiga antelope and musk oxen. Their forests and grasslands were home to aurochs and bison, while chamois and goats inhabited the rocky heights.

In contrast, the Neanderthals stuck close to their evergreen forests of holm oak and cork oak, without Arctic fauna and perhaps without bison. Their ecological equilibrium was upset when the wave of cold blowing over Europe penetrated deep into the confines of Iberia, drastically affecting the Mediterranean ecosystems and effectively destroying the world of the last Iberian Neanderthals. As the Cro-Magnons of the steppes swept down into southern Europe in the wake of this climatic change, the last Neanderthals probably withdrew to milder lowlands near the sea.

34   The first Neanderthals to use tools for hunting
   A   populated south-west Asia and the Middle East.
   B   discovered ivory and other animal products.
   C   inhabited areas near those occupied by Cro-Magnons.
   D   adapted to warmer climates about 100,000 years ago.

35   What was a key factor in the Cro-Magnons surviving the pre-glacial cold in Europe?
   A   learning from the Neanderthals
   B   discovering deep caves where they could live
   C   building shelters to stay warm in
   D   their ability to communicate effectively

36   It is likely that early forms of jewellery
   A   also served the purpose of keeping humans warm.
   B   allowed humans to distinguish what roles they had within their society.
   C   were the first steps towards modern culture.
   D   led to humans forming well-organised tribes.

37   When did the Neanderthals migrate to the Russian Plain?
   A   as soon as conditions allowed them to reach 52 degrees north
   B   when there was nowhere else for them to go
   C   between the last two glacial periods
   D   just before the temperatures began to rise

38   During the last Ice Age, the Cro-Magnons first built shelters when
   A   the temperatures were at their lowest.
   B   they could find enough mammoth bones.
   C   they discovered new supplies of fuel.
   D   there weren't enough caves for them to live in.

39   Why did Cro-Magnons choose to live in the north of the Iberian Peninsula?
   A   They feared the Neanderthals to the south.
   B   There were caves where they could seek refuge.
   C   The landscape was similar to where they had come from.
   D   They were too tired to move further south.

40   The Cro-Magnons moved to southern Europe
   A   at the same time as the Neanderthals died out.
   B   when the lowlands became flooded.
   C   before they ran short of food.
   D   shortly after a great climatic change.

Test Four

Paper 2: Writing

Part 1

You must answer this question. Write your answer in **300-350** words in an appropriate style.

1. You work as a journalist for an English language newspaper in your country. A reader has sent in a letter which included the extract below. Your editor has asked you to write an article on the subject brought up in the letter, commenting on the points raised and adding your own views on the subject.

> It has recently come to light that a substantial number of artefacts in museums and galleries are being stored away from public view in unsuitable conditions, causing them to succumb to the effects of chemicals in the air, humidity and insects. These institutions simply do not have the resources to maintain so many exhibits. Should the artefacts then, for the sake of posterity, be sold off to private collectors who would lovingly care for them and provide sorely-needed finances for museums and galleries?

Write your **article**.

Part 2

Write an answer to one of the questions **2-4** in this part. Write your answer in **300-350** words in an appropriate style.

2. You work for a travel agency and have just returned from the maiden voyage of a luxury cruise liner around the Mediterranean. Your boss has asked you to write a report on the facilities on the liner and the places visited on the cruise.

   Write your **report**.

3. You have recently returned from an arts festival where you attended several poetry and music recitals and saw several films and plays. You thoroughly enjoyed the festival and you were astonished to read a poor review of it in a newspaper. Write a letter to the newspaper criticising the review and clearly stating why the festival did not deserve such a harsh review.

   Write your **letter**.

4. Because the health club you work for has been losing members to competitors in the same area, a large sum of money has been made available to improve its facilities. Your manager has asked you to write a proposal on how best to spend the money in order to attract more members.

   Write your **proposal**.

Hints on writing a proposal

A proposal is something like a report in that a similar format is used. However, while a report is backward focusing, in that it says what has happened, a proposal focuses on the future. It is primarily to make suggestions and recommendations for discussion.

For example, one such task could be a youth club which wants to be awarded a government grant for improvements to its facilities. The proposal would have to include details of how, if awarded the money, the club would spend the money, the benefits the money would offer the club and how the club's progress could be monitored if it were awarded the money.

A proposal should be well structured and the different sections clearly identified. It is best to use section headings for this reason. Ideas need to be presented in well-organised prose and paragraphing and use of linking devices should be evident.

It is important to think about who the target reader is and use the appropriate register. As this is likely to be a proposal in some kind of business situation, a formal register will normally be appropriate.

Paper 3: Use of English

Hints on sentence transformation (Part 4)

There are eight sentences in this part of the **Use of English** paper. On the first line there is a complete sentence and below it you are given a key word. You have to use this word, in the form it is given, to complete a second sentence so that it has a similar meaning to the first one. You must use between three and eight words.

Read the original sentence carefully and then look at the given word and the gapped sentence. Think about what is being tested.

For example:

> I have had no one to keep me company all day.
>
> **own**
>
> I ....*have been on my own*........ all day.

In this example, you are being tested to see if you confuse *on my own* and *by myself*. In addition, you need to know that you must change the verb *have had* to *have been*.

All questions involve making two changes to the lead-in sentence. Each change is worth one mark. The transformation involves a change in focus. For example, you may be required to make a personal construction impersonal, or a positive one negative.

Sometimes you may be required to make a change in the tense used (eg, from present perfect to simple past). Taking note of time expressions can help you in this.

Commonly tested areas:

- Remember that inversion is frequently tested in this exercise, as it is in other parts of the exam.
- With reported speech you need to check that you have moved the verb back a tense and that you have used the correct word order.

    For example:

    > 'Did you see Sarah yesterday?' I asked him.
    >
    > **if**
    >
    > I asked him ....*if he had seen Sarah*........ yesterday.

- Some of the other areas that may be tested are:
    - active to passive
    - change of subject
    - comparatives and superlatives
    - *only, except for, apart from*
    - conditionals
    - *so/such*
    - collocations

These are only a few of the grammatical areas you could be tested on, so revise any structure you have problems with.

When you have written your new sentence, read it through carefully. Is it as similar in meaning as possible to the original sentence? Is your use of prepositions correct? Check your spelling too. Is your sentence in the same tense as the original or do you have a good reason for shifting tenses? Have you remembered to include emphasis that might have been part of the original sentence?

Test Four

Part 1

For questions **1-15**, read the text below and think of the word which best fits each space. Use only one word in each space. There is an example at the beginning (**0**).

Example: | **0** | FROM |

Walking disposal units

On returning (0) ....**FROM**.... a visit to America in 1847, a Norwegian lawyer reported many differences between Europe and the land on the other (1) .... of the Atlantic. What struck him (2) .... really odd, however, was the ubiquitous American pig. During his stay, he observed that pigs kept the streets clean by eating up all (3) .... of refuse. Then, when these walking disposal units were full, they were butchered and provided a real treat for the dinner table. They were the original recycling units.

Working class women, who (4) .... on the pigs to supply food for the table, allowed them to roam (5) .... they wanted in order to scavenge for garbage. Thus, city pigs converted waste into protein for the working poor. But as the saying (6) .... , one man's meat is another man's poison, and by 1848 (7) .... many pigs were wandering the streets that they began to be seen as a nuisance (8) .... some. Occasionally, they injured or (9) .... killed children.

(10) .... response, the authorities tried to ban the animals from roaming the streets, but a public outcry led to the act (11) .... repealed. It wasn't (12) .... 1849, when cholera broke (13) .... in New York and the pig was blamed for causing the filthy conditions in (14) .... the disease thrives, that the urban pig began to disappear. Finally, it was banished to the farmyard and today it symbolises the division between the (15) .... and the city.

Part 2

For questions **16-25**, read the text below. Use the word given in capitals at the end of some of the lines to form a word that fits in the space in the same line. There is an example at the beginning (**0**).

Example: | **0** | WORRYING |

Fussy eaters

If there is one thing that is likely to be (0) ....**WORRYING**.... for first-time parents, it is a	WORRY
young child's eating problems. Most of these parents' worries, however, are	
(16) .... since the incidence of children who do not enjoy their food	FOUND
is far more (17) .... than the majority imagine and the retention	SPREAD
beyond (18) .... of such problems to adolescence is	CHILD
(19) .... rare.	COMPARE
There are, of course, case which have persisted into adulthood and those which appear	
to be more than just a (20) .... phase. In these cases, professional	PASS
(21) .... has to be sought.	GUIDE
Up to now, psychiatrists have (22) .... nine distinct types of eating	CATEGORY
(23) .... , each with its own particular treatment. The least serious of these	ORDER
is selective eating, when the child displays an (24) .... to try anything but a	WILL
narrow range of foods. This affects about 12% of three-year-olds but it rarely persists. The	
most serious is persuasive refusal syndrome, which affects only a (25) .... of	HAND
people and requires psychiatric supervision and treatment.	

91

Paper 3: Use of English

Part 3

For questions **26-31**, think of one word only which can be used appropriately in all three sentences. Here is an example (**0**).

Example:

0 With its .... soil, the area near the volcano is prime agricultural land.
Being difficult to digest, ... food is best avoided late at night.
I smelt the .... aroma of freshly-ground coffee as I walked in the door.

| **0** | RICH |

26 They formed a .... around the burglar to prevent him from escaping.
Although she had lied in the past, her explanation had more than a .... of truth about it.
Moving cautiously around the .... , the boxers probed each other's defence.

27 He was arrested because he .... to the description of the wanted man.
I wish I hadn't .... the door when a salesman came to my house yesterday.
She .... an advertisement in the personal column and is now married to the man who placed it.

28 The guest house offers only half ....
The .... of directors have arranged to meet to discuss the possibility of expanding the business.
Always check the bulletin .... for situations vacant.

29 A practical joker, James likes nothing more than to creep up behind people and make them ....
It's difficult to follow the train of thought of a lecturer who tends to .... from one subject to another.
Most people would .... at the chance of meeting a famous person.

30 As there was little margarine left, we had to .... it thinly on the bread.
News of the scandal .... so quickly that by lunchtime everyone knew about it.
The officers involved in the search for the murder weapon were told to .... out while scouring the field.

31 The clear blue sky promised .... weather for the rest of the day.
The twins' hair couldn't have been more different: Jane's was dark and Sue's was ....
Ronald didn't think it was .... of his parents to let his older brother go out while he had to stay at home.

Part 4

For questions **32-39**, complete the second sentence so that it has a similar meaning to the first sentence, using the word given. **Do not change the word given**. You must use between **three** and **eight** words, including the word given. Here is an example (**0**).

Example:

0 They are determined to enter the tournament although they are not fully fit.

intent

They .... for the tournament although they are not fully fit.

| are intent on going in |

32 It was impossible for Joe to accept that he would never get another job.

terms

Joe .... fact that he would be unemployed from now on.

33 When it comes to pronouncing long words, Maria has definitely improved in the past few months.

been

There .... of long words in the past few months.

34 It is extremely important never to let the situation get out of control.

remain

You .... all times.

35 None of us expected Mr White to recover so quickly.

aback

We .... of Mr White's recovery.

36 I firmly believe that Veronica had no idea where the missing jewellery was.

knowledge

It is my .... the whereabouts of the missing jewellery.

37 There has been a huge increase in property prices recently.

roof

Property prices .... recently.

38 Stan claims he has been successful because he is well-educated.

puts

Stan .... education.

39 She asked the passengers not to smoke until they had left the aeroplane.

refrain

She asked the passengers .... until they had left the aeroplane.

Paper 3: Use of English

Part 5

For questions **40-44**, read the following texts on stress. For questions **40-43**, answer with a word or short phrase. You do not need to write complete sentences. For question **44**, write a summary according to the instructions given.

> Unless you have been isolated from society for the past two decades, you will have heard the word 'stress'. But what does it actually mean? I'll wager that if you ask ten individuals this question, you'll get ten different answers. Strange, you may think, that such a common word could have so many different definitions, but you would be mistaken. Just as the idea of what constitutes love is likely to provoke
> 5 disagreement, so the same applies to stress.
>
> Although we often tend to think of stress as being externally induced, events occurring in our lives are not stressful in themselves. What causes stress is the way we interpret and react to them. Consequently, there is a dramatic variation in responses to potentially stressful situations and a corresponding variation in how stress can be overcome. Despite this lack of uniformity, there are certain events we
> 10 experience which are normally associated with stress.
>
> Stress-provoking situations can be generally divided into two categories: life changes and environmental events. The first category includes a change in marital status, a change of career, workplace, address, or educational establishment and the loss of a loved one. As regards environmental events, time constraints, financial problems and noise are the basic factors responsible for sowing the
> 15 seeds of stress. Unfortunately, there is no universal panacea for dealing with stress, but the first step towards minimising its effects is to become aware of its presence.

40 In the second paragraph, what point about how we are affected by stress does the writer make?
....

41 Explain in your own words how the writer says we can begin to confront the problem of stress.
....

94

Test Four

Stress is the term used to describe the physical and emotional rigours our bodies undergo when we adapt to changes in our lives. Contrary to popular belief, stress can produce positive responses as well as the well-documented adverse symptoms. Positive stress, as it is known, can spur us on to greater heights by increasing awareness which, in turn, helps us to lead a fuller, more satisfying life. Unfortunately, though, any benefits that stress may bring very often give way to the darker effects of negative stress.

Far from producing a feeling of well-being, negative stress induces a range of unpleasant mental, behavioural and physiological reactions. Basically, its victims suffer from low self-esteem due to an inability to achieve set goals. This results primarily in a fear of further failure. Outwardly, people exposed to extremely stressful situations display distinct patterns of behaviour. They become increasingly impulsive, more heavily dependent on nicotine, drugs or alcohol and excessively prone to overeating. The upshot of all this is that unrelieved stress causes sweating, an increased heartbeat rate, sleeping problems and inexplicable tiredness.

This list alone is enough to heighten anxiety even if you are not stressed out, but advice is not in short supply for those who are. Although what they advise is not equally applicable to every person negatively affected by stress, there are some useful standard recommendations. Any strategy for tackling stress should begin with actually recognising there is a problem rather than denying it. When the root of the problem has been identified, it is time to react. This involves pinpointing ways of modifying or changing the factors responsible for it. Finally, action needs to be taken to reduce the intensity of the stressors. There is a host of tactics available at this stage, each of which is designed to alleviate stress to differing degrees. These include shortening exposure to stressors, moderating physical reactions to them and building physical reserves which can provide protection against them through regular exercise.

42 Explain in your own words the meaning of the expression 'spur us on to greater heights'. (line 3)

43 Which phrase in paragraph 3 echoes the idea that 'there is no universal panacea for dealing with stress' expressed in the first text.

44 In a paragraph of between **50 and 70** words, summarise **in your own words as far as possible**, what causes stress and how can it be alleviated according to the information given in the texts.

Test Four

Paper 4: Listening

Hints on how to decide which speaker said what (Part 4)

In this type of exercise, you are given two speakers to choose from and the texts are always of a conversational nature. The testing focus will be on what was said and on whether or not speakers are in agreement on certain points. You should be listening for what the speakers express through their intonation and choice of idiom, as well as through what is directly stated. Most of the time, the speakers' agreement or disagreement is implied, not explicitly stated. You will rarely hear a speaker say, 'Yes, you're right' or 'I agree'.

The questions generally follow the order of the passage you are listening to.

Read the instructions carefully so that you know exactly how to answer. You will have to use the first letter of each of the speakers' names to indicate which speaker said something and B for both, if they both agree on a given opinion or view.

Use the time given to you to read the statements through carefully before the cassette is played. These will not be the exact words you will hear on the tape, so listen carefully. Answer whatever you can on the first listening, then on the second listening complete any answers you are not sure about and check your other answers.

When you transfer your answers on to the answer sheet, ensure that your handwriting is clear and legible so that the examiner can read your answer.

Test Four

Part 1

You will hear four different extracts. For questions 1-8, choose the answer (**A**, **B**, or **C**) which fits best according to what you hear. There are two questions for each extract.

Extract One

You hear a woman talking about her childhood trips to Italy.

1 Why was the woman surprised to see a shoemaker?
    A   She had thought all shoes were mass-produced.
    B   She didn't know they made shoes in Italy.
    C   She didn't think anyone knew how to make shoes any more.

2 Why did the speaker expect the shoes to be expensive?
    A   Because they were made of leather.
    B   Because it was difficult for Giovanni to make shoes.
    C   Because each pair was unique.

Extract Two

You hear a man making a speech in acceptance of an award.

3 How did the speaker feel about accepting the award?
    A   extremely proud
    B   slightly embarrassed
    C   a little afraid

4 Why did he thank his family?
    A   They had been with him during filming.
    B   They had been supportive of him while he was working.
    C   They had worked hard while he was filming.

Extract Three

You hear a woman talking about cosmetic surgery

5 What is the speaker's general view of cosmetic surgery?
    A   Sometimes radical changes are necessary.
    B   It can enhance one's appearance.
    C   Only people with serious imperfections ought to try it.

6 How does the speaker justify the money she spent?
    A   It was money she'd spent on herself.
    B   It wasn't a lot anyway.
    C   It was money she'd earned herself.

Extract Four

You hear a man talking about his work.

7 Why does he think his only alternative would be unemployment?
    A   He has only worked on production lines.
    B   His age is against him.
    C   He can't do many tasks.

8 Why isn't it possible to hear the music in the factory?
    A   The machines drown out the sound.
    B   The music isn't piped to every part of the factory.
    C   Everyone is shouting.

Test Four

Paper 4: Listening

Part 2

You will hear a radio report about driver ants. For questions **9-17**, complete the sentences with a word or short phrase.

You can often find over [____9____] ants in some colonies.

The method that army ants use to collect food and the [____10____] they need is interesting.

Army ants gather food in [____11____]

Whilst looking for food, worker ants rush over the ground or along [____12____]

When making swarm raids, the ants [____13____] along the ground in a net-like pattern.

The [____15____] of a swarming ant is more powerful than that of a column raider.

To protect themselves in a flood, driver ant colonies group together in [____14____] with the soldier ants on the outside.

Army ants have unusual nests that are constructed out of [____16____]

One advantage of having army ants in your house would be the fact that you would not be bothered by other [____17____]

Test Four

Part 3

You will hear an interview with language expert, Ryan, who recently researched the opportunities to learn a foreign language via the Internet. For questions **18-22**, choose the answer (**A**, **B**, **C** or **D**) which fits best according to what you hear.

18 What is Ryan's general view of the Internet?
   A It should only be used to supplement traditional language classes.
   B It's a valuable but unusual source of educational help.
   C It's worth more than we pay for it.
   D It should be more centralised.

19 Ryan thinks chat rooms are helpful to language students
   A as a replacement to conventional studies.
   B as a place to ask people about grammar or vocabulary.
   C when used alongside academic studies.
   D because they provide them with new friends.

20 What does Ryan think is the most helpful way for language students to use a chat room?
   A one-to-one chat
   B observation
   C participation in conversations
   D talking to teachers

21 What does Ryan say about foreign radio and TV stations?
   A They have language learning programmes.
   B Foreign students appear on them.
   C They can also aid language learning.
   D They aren't available via the Internet.

22 What does Ryan believe about using the Internet to aid language learning?
   A It will make the classroom obsolete.
   B It will become more and more important.
   C It will replace studying abroad.
   D It isn't useful for everyone.

Part 4

You will hear two people, Audrey and William, talking about wind power. For questions **23-28**, decide whether the opinions are expressed by only one of the speakers, or whether the speakers agree.

Write **A**   for Audrey
      W   for William
or   **B**   for Both, where they agree.

23 New energy sources must be found immediately.

24 We can't ignore wind power as a viable energy source.

25 Wind farms are clean, pollution-free energy providers.

26 Plans are adapted according to the results of consultations.

27 People are initially uncertain about wind farms.

28 The construction of wind farms can provide local employment.

Test Four

Paper 5: Speaking

Part 1

- How do you usually spend your weekends?
- What kind of area do you live in?
- Are the entertainment facilities in your area adequate?
- Do you prefer going to the cinema or the theatre?
- If you could, what would you change about your education or career?
- Are there any skills that you would like to learn?
- What are the employment opportunities like in this area?

Part 2

Here are some pictures depicting people involved in different aspects of music production. (Page 173)

a First I'd like you to look at pictures A and B and talk together about what feelings and emotions the people featured might be experiencing. You have one minute to do this.

b Now, I'd like you to look at all the pictures. Imagine that a poster is being designed for a music festival which will be held in your city. Talk together about how appropriate you feel each photo is and recommend two more types of music.

You have three minutes to talk about this.

Part 3

In this part of the test you are going to talk on your own for about two minutes. You need to listen while your partner is speaking because you'll be asked to comment afterwards.

I'm going to give you a card with a question on it and I'd like you to say what you think. There are some ideas on the card for you to use if you want.

Candidate A, here is your card.

Prompt Card A

> How important is music in the world today?
> - expressing feelings
> - culture
> - social life

Candidate B, is there anything you don't agree with? (1 minute)
Candidates A and B, how important is it for all young people to learn to play a musical instrument? (1 minute)

Candidate B, look at your card and say what you think.

Prompt Card B

> What is more important – traditional music or modern music?
> - reminder of the past
> - developing new ideas
> - innovation versus resistance to change

Candidate A, is there anything you would like to add? (1 minute)
Candidates A and B, what is the best form of entertainment for young people today? (1 minute)

Both candidates: Now to finish the test, we are going to talk about entertainment. (4 minutes)

- Is it a good thing that synthesizers are replacing the need for musical ability in modern music?
- How are attitudes to entertainment in modern society changing?
- How important is live theatre?
- Will DVDs replace the cinema as a form of entertainment?

Test Four

Hints on how to respond to written questions (Part 3)

In this part of the Speaking paper, each candidate is required to answer a question which is on a card. The card also has some ideas to help you. When it is your turn to answer, take full advantage of these prompts, as they are a very good starting point. You are expected to speak for about two minutes on the subject.

While the other candidate is answering their question, be sure to listen carefully, as you must comment on what they say when they have finished. The interlocutor will ask you if there is anything you would like to add. Although it may seem as if you can choose not to add anything at this point, remember that you will lose marks if you don't contribute.

Practise using some of the following:

> That's exactly what I think.
> I quite agree.
> I suppose ...
> That may be so, but ...
> I'm not sure I agree with you.
> I don't agree.

When you have both answered your questions, you will both be asked other, more general questions on the subject you have just spoken about.

Remember that it is the language you use which is the most important thing, not your knowledge of the particular subject. Give your opinion in the best English you can, and don't worry too much about how much (or little) you know about the subject in question.

101

Test Five

Paper 1: Reading

Hints on improving your chances

It is essential that you read as many English books, newspapers and magazines as you can in order to improve your chances in Paper 1 of the Cambridge Certificate of Proficiency in English examination.

Don't just rely on learning the words and phrases you come across in class. You need to make the extra effort to read outside the classroom and to record and learn words and phrases systematically.

This will serve a number of purposes. Not only will you expand your vocabulary, but you will also speed up your ability to read and understand the gist of a passage in English. This will be particularly helpful when it comes to dealing with Part 3 and Part 4 of the Reading paper where there are large texts to get through.

Remember to answer every question, even if you have no idea what the correct answer is. You have more chance of getting the answer right by guessing than if you just leave a blank.

Test Five

Part 1

For questions 1-18, read the three texts below and decide which answer (**A**, **B**, **C**, or **D**) best fits each gap.

SURVIVING AGAINST THE ODDS

How is it possible for a person to stop breathing for an hour underwater and yet survive, while others (1) .... in just a few centimetres of water? The answer is simple: cold water. When a person plunges into icy water, the body temperature (2) .... rapidly due to super-fast cooling, causing blood to move to (3) .... organs from other parts of the body. Soon, hypothermia (4) .... and the lungs fill with water, making the body appear lifeless.

To the (5) .... eye, a hypothermic victim in this state may appear to be beyond help. But CPR administered by those first on the scene, and continued until they are (6) .... by professionals, can make the difference between life and death. Survivors have gone on to live quite normal lives when resuscitation attempts have been successful.

1	A	choke	B	suffocate	C	drown	D	asphyxiate
2	A	falls	B	reduces	C	lessens	D	dwindles
3	A	vital	B	essential	C	significant	D	fundamental
4	A	comes up	B	takes over	C	sets in	D	brings round
5	A	uneducated	B	untrained	C	illiterate	D	uninformed
6	A	overtaken	B	relinquished	C	exchanged	D	relieved

MY BOSS AMANDA

Amanda was headstrong. Of that there could be no doubt. She was also rather intolerant of anyone who dared oppose her, confronting them with sarcasm and (7) .... comments whenever they did not take the (8) .... that she was loathe to have her decisions questioned.

I, too, was subjected to the occasional tongue-lashing, but far from being intimidated, I actually found the experience invigorating. I know this is not everyone's (9) .... of stimulation, but as I fancied myself as a bit of an amateur psychologist, I saw it as a challenge to try and find out why she (10) .... in these verbal assaults.

As I (11) .... her life through a combination of office gossip and a little simple detective work, I discovered that her parents were domineering to say the least. She was constantly nagged at home, where nothing she did seemed to (12) .... with her parents' approval. Her only outlet was her staff, on whom she vented her anger and frustration.

7	A	cutting	B	splitting	C	piercing	D	throbbing
8	A	note	B	suggestion	C	clue	D	hint
9	A	perception	B	feeling	C	thought	D	idea
10	A	entered	B	engaged	C	occupied	D	attended
11	A	sorted out	B	spied on	C	delved into	D	filtered through
12	A	fit	B	find	C	meet	D	take

RECORDING BABYLON

Ever since Herodotus (13) .... at the city of Babylon, the legends which surround the long-lost wonders of the ancient world have been passed down from generation to generation. These stories have fascinated people from all (14) .... of life for centuries, but it wasn't until the early 20th century that serious excavation work began to uncover the secrets buried beneath the desert sands.

Still in progress today, this archaeological dig has been (15) .... slow due to problems that have arisen with the clay tablets on which Babylonian history is recorded in ancient writing. Clay tablets are more resistant to the (16) .... of time than papyrus, but when they are removed from their resting place, exposing them to the atmosphere, they crumble. Thus, there is a (17) .... against time to avoid losing their contents forever. Using a holographic process, scientists are able to print a 3D image of the tablet on a glass plate before it is reduced to dust. In this way, technology has been able to assist archaeologists in preserving the (18) .... of Nebuchadnezzar and shed more light on Babylonian life.

13	A	engrossed	B	admired	C	enthused	D	marvelled
14	A	paths	B	courses	C	walks	D	routes
15	A	absolutely	B	painfully	C	utterly	D	extensively
16	A	casualties	B	ravages	C	damages	D	disturbances
17	A	race	B	match	C	game	D	sprint
18	A	inheritance	B	legacy	C	heirloom	D	keepsake

103

Test Five

Paper 1: Reading

Part 2

You are going to read four extracts which are all concerned in some way with the body. For questions **19-26**, choose the answer (**A**, **B**, **C** or **D**) which you think fits best according to the text.

Green light for skin grafts

Nowadays skin grafts are commonplace in cosmetic surgery as well as in procedures performed on burn victims, where a successful graft can mean the difference between life and death. Existing methods involve stitching, stapling or using tissue glues to secure the graft, but threads and staples sometimes cause extensive scarring while chemical glues can trigger inflammation.

These unwelcome problems may soon become a thing of the past if recent tests using laser-activated glue fulfil the promise they have shown so far. These tests involved placing two layers of pig skin together, with a thin layer of medical dye in between. To bond the two layers, the skin was illuminated with green light for fifteen minutes.

The bond between the layers became fifteen times as strong after being exposed to laser light, which made it twice as strong as bonds created with standard glues. Crucially, the laser only heated the skin slightly above body temperature, leaving the surrounding tissue completely undamaged. The only drawback to the procedure is that it is slow, but a more powerful laser driving much faster bonding could overcome that.

19 What is the main advantage of bonding with green light?
   A The bond lasts much longer.
   B It can be used more easily on burn victims.
   C Any type of skin can be used.
   D It leaves no evidence of a skin graft.

20 What causes the new method to be successful?
   A the temperature at which bonding occurs
   B the thickness of the bonding layer
   C the unlimited area of skin that can be grafted
   D the low cost of the procedure

Early diagnosis

A cheap and easy blood test has been developed to help reduce the number of people dying from heart disease by detecting the earliest signs of furry arteries. The test, which requires only a few drops of blood, would be a welcome replacement for the best method available at present, an angiogram. This method involves injecting a contrast-enhancing chemical into individual blood vessels before X-raying them, which is expensive, time-consuming and risky.

The new technique relies on measuring the concentration of metabolites, small molecules such as fatty acids that are formed or used in metabolism. In people with heart problems, the body is fighting against disease and this will show up in the concentration of metabolites present in the blood sample. The analysis is carried out by placing blood plasma in an NMR (nuclear magnetic resonance) machine. This subjects the sample to a magnetic field and a quick blast of radio waves which make the protons in the nuclei of the molecules vibrate. The frequencies and intensity of the radio waves that are sent out by the vibrating protons determine which metabolites are present in the sample together with their concentration.

The technique, called metabonomics, could also be used to diagnose many other conditions, such as bone and brain diseases.

21 The new blood test relies on the fact that
   A angiograms are potentially dangerous.
   B blood vessels can be clearly seen on X-rays.
   C metabolites cause arteries to become furry.
   D the body of a person suffering from heart disease is in a state of defence.

22 During the analysis of the blood sample
   A the NMR machine vibrates causing a structural change in metabolites.
   B spinning blood plasma creates a unique magnetic field.
   C vibration of protons leads to a change in metabolite concentration.
   D the effect of radio wave frequencies on metabolites is measured.

Test Five

A distant cousin

Genomes are now coming in thick and fast, each one providing valuable information about the evolutionary jigsaw puzzle of life on Earth. The seventh to be sequenced, that of the sea squirt, *Cionia intestinalis,* is no exception. It is thought that the genome of this creature, a distant cousin of animals with backbones, is helping determine how the genome of vertebrates like us evolved.

Sea squirts, with their leathery filter-feeding tubes, do not resemble long-lost relatives, but the larval form of sea squirts reveals its true ancestry. These free-swimming tadpoles have a stiffened rod or notochord running down their back, which in a developing vertebrate is a forerunner to the backbone. They also have a simple brain and a heart.

The creature that gave rise to both the sea squirt and vertebrates appeared during the Cambrian explosion, an orgy of evolutionary experimentation about 550 million years ago. Since modern sea squirts are thought to be similar to this common ancestor, comparing their genome with ours reveals how the vertebrate genome evolved.

A second more surprising finding concerns an unexpected gene detected during the sequencing of the genome. It appears that *Cionia* has stolen at least one gene from bacteria. This gene enables it to make a cellulose-like compound that forms a protective leathery tunic and is found in no other animal.

23 Why, at first sight, would *Cionia intestinalis* seem unlikely to provide clues about the origin of vertebrates?
   A It has larvae found in no other species.
   B It looks nothing like a vertebrate.
   C It lives in a marine environment.
   D There are so many different species of this animal.

24 The genome of *Cionia* has revealed that
   A its ancestor did not resemble a sea squirt.
   B it has acquired genetic material from an unlikely source.
   C the presence of cellulose played an important part in its evolution.
   D sequencing is becoming increasingly difficult.

Close relationships

Have you every heard of *Demodex folliculorum*, a 0.4-millimetre mite and a member of the extended family of the spider? Probably not, but if you squint, you can get a close-up of one of its preferred habitats. The eyelash mite, as it is more commonly known, lives on almost everybody's face, feeding on dead skin cells and often burrowing into eyelash follicles. And that is not the only creature we share our bodies with. A veritable menagerie of microbes inhabits our various nooks and crannies. Spirochetes live in our gums; while *staphylococci, micrococci* and a small yeast from the genus *Pityrosporon* clothe our hides. And then, of course, there is the gut, home to species of bacteria that provide us with, among other things, some of our daily quota of B12 and K vitamins. In fact, there are so many co-inhabitants of our bodies that it has been estimated that a staggering 10% of our dry weight is made up not of our own cells, but of our symbionts.

Do these facts surprise you? Maybe not, but their implications probably escape the vast majority. The natural world is full of similar situations that have led to some startling assertions. If we look at the simplest level of life, the single-celled organism, close inspection reveals that certain bacteria are sometimes 'body-farmed' to act as a defence organ. Neither the organism nor its bacterial bodyguard can survive alone, so it can be concluded that this life form clearly evolved when one genome acquired the other. If we take this one step further, we can see that our evolution has been, to an extent, shaped by the unsung heroes of symbiology that share our bodies and are indeed part of us.

25 What does the writer imply about 'the gut' in line 12?
   A It contains a host of microbes.
   B Most of its weight is made up of bacteria.
   C The way it functions resembles a single-cell organism.
   D More research needs to be done on it.

26 How does the writer regard the human body?
   A as a piece of machinery
   B as an ecosystem
   C as a rapidly evolving organism
   D as a marvel of genetic engineering

Paper 1: Reading

Part 3

You are going to read an article about electric paper. Seven paragraphs have been removed from the article. Choose from the paragraphs **A–H** the one which best fits each gap (**27–33**). There is one extra paragraph which you do not need to use.

Tired of staring at the same four walls? Cream is so 1990s. Would a lick of paint help? Don't reach for the brush just yet. With electronic wallpaper, your chameleon-like walls would change to suit the mood or occasion. Flick a switch and watch as cream wallpaper transforms itself into fashionable terracotta. Flick it again and the room changes to brilliant green. You'll never need to lift a paintbrush again.

27

Scientists have been trying to modernise paper for decades. Most research so far has concentrated on replacing paper with other materials such as plastic and glass. Companies like Gyricon Media in Silicon Valley and E-ink in Cambridge, Massachusetts now offer relatively cheap paper substitutes made of plastic for personal organisers and advertisements. But these substitutes miss one simple point: people like paper.

28

Paper does have one major disadvantage, though: once text or an image is printed, you can't change it. It's a weakness that Gyrican and E-ink are exploiting with their electronic 'paper'. But what if you could transform normal, run-of-the-mill paper into electronic displays?

29

Their current display is an 'active matrix' similar to the thin-film transistor (TFT) screens found in laptops. Each pixel on a laptop screen is made of a liquid crystal display cell connected to a transistor, which controls the voltage across the cell, its chemical properties and hence its colour. Most screens, including TFTs, rely on expensive silicon electronics, but the Scandinavian team makes both the transistors and display cells by printing semi-conducting polymers onto paper.

30

With just 40 pixels, each slightly larger that a postage stamp, Berggren's display hardly competes with TFT screens, but it is proof that paper electronic displays do work. The real application of the technology, Berggren stresses, is huge low-resolution displays. His team has already demonstrated a seven-segment display similar to a digital clock.

31

There are still some hurdles to overcome though. At present, each pixel takes around five seconds to update. As the speed of the chemical reaction is inversely proportional to the cell area, a pixel as large as a poster or a strip of wall paper would take anything from minutes up to several hours to change hue. This shouldn't be a problem for advertisements that are updated overnight, but it might limit other uses.

32

More pressing than pretty colours is a power supply. At the moment, the power comes from batteries connected to the paper with crocodile clips which obviously won't work for magazines or cereal packets. Because the displays operate at such low voltages, the team is thinking about using radio waves to transmit power over less than a metre, or attaching flexible, printable batteries. In the latter option, chemical inks act as the anode and cathode and can produce up to 15 volts, which is enough to run the paper displays.

33

Back at home, your livid green walls still don't look right. Overwhelmed by choice, with a rainbow of colours available at the flick of a switch, a return to cream seems the only sensible choice. Like our inability to give up paper after some two thousand years, old habits die hard.

A And they have bigger plans. They're aiming to create poster-sized displays for shops, flashing cereal boxes and packaging for toys and, within three to five years, even changing text in magazines. Although the technology is still in its infancy, companies, including the advertising giant JCDecaux, which owns over 600,000 billboards in 40 countries, are beginning to take notice.

B Another difficulty is that the colour is no match for the bright hues of computer screens. Berggren admits that commercial printers describe his displays as 'terrible'. So in order to compete, the team will need polymers that produce magenta, cyan, black and yellow, the primary colours used in printing. Progress in this area has been made and a complex polymer that can turn yellow has already been found.

C That's exactly what Berggren and his colleagues at Linköping University and the Advanced Centre for Research in Electronics and Optics in Norrköping, Sweden, have been doing. Four years ago, they asked paper makers whether they'd like more from their newspaper and packaging by adding electronic circuits, sensors and displays, also made from paper. The response was overwhelming and last year the researchers unveiled an electronic display printed on standard paper. Eventually, they hope to develop the technology that will enable them to convert any piece of paper into a fully functioning display.

D Whatever the power source, there are two good reasons why electronic paper might just take off. Firstly, if the printing is done using industrial reel-to-reel processes, it will cost only a couple of euros per square metre. Secondly, you can throw it in the recycling bin when you've finished with it.

E For indecisive home improvers who are forever changing their rooms, high-tech decorations like these are on their way. Last year, Magnus Berggren of Linköping University in Sweden and his team printed cheap, electronic displays on paper, paving the way for moving images, changing colours and text on everything from wallpaper to milk cartons and advertising billboards.

F The display exploits the unusual electrochemical properties of poly (3, 4-ethylenedioxythiophene) or PEDOT. Pixels made from this transparent polymer turn blue when a voltage is applied. When the voltage is reversed, the pixels become clear again. The chemical reactions behind this transformation are 'bi-stable'. This means that to flip the polymers from one state to the other, only a voltage needs to be applied when the information needs updating.

G Paper has survived the test of time because you can write and draw anything you like on it, fold it up and put it in your pocket. And unlike an electronic screen, you can read a newspaper from any angle in bright sunlight. Paper also feels good and, above all, it is cheap to make in huge quantities. Every year, the global paper industry churns out nearly 320 million tonnes of the stuff.

H To overlay the transistors with display cells, Berggren then passes the paper through a laminator, which covers it with a layer of plastic peppered with holes. Using another screen printer, he then fills these holes with an electrolyte similar to the liquid found in car batteries. This allows a final layer of PEDOT to react chemically when a voltage is applied to the electrodes. The final step involves laminating the paper again, this time with a thin plastic foil made of PEDOT. The end product feels like glossy inkjet paper.

Paper 1: Reading

Part 4

You are going to read an article on Monaco. For questions **34-40**, choose the answer (**A**, **B**, **C**, or **D**) which you think fits best according to the text.

MONACO'S BRITISH

From a sprawling penthouse overlooking the port crowded with luxury yachts, the two faces of Monaco can be contemplated. First, there is the picturesque old town and the white and red castle perched on a rock regally surveying the Mediterranean below. In the other direction, there is the uglier face of the independent principality, every available yard covered with council-style tower blocks to house the richest tax avoiders in the world. Within these blocks live the growing influx of Britons, who now number 5000 – three times as many as ten years ago.

The expatriate population, with its own schools, pubs, clubs, radio station and cricket team is steadily taking control of this narrow enclave's social life, just as it did in the nineteenth century when British aristocrats and newly-rich industrialists flocked to the attractions around Europe's first casino at Monte Carlo. At its current growth rate, the British colony, lured by tax breaks and easier residency conditions, may soon surpass the 6000 native Monegasques and a similar number of Italians. However, it will take them much longer to overtake the French who, among their other privileges, run the 400-strong police force that makes the mini-territory of 340,000 bank accounts virtually crime-free.

The reason for expatriates flooding to Monaco is abundantly clear but how exactly do they spend their time in the tax haven? What constitutes a typical day for the recently wealthy expatriates following in the footsteps of Greek shipowners, Arab oil millionaires and Middle Eastern Jewish financiers who provided the post-war capital that turned the sleepy seaside rock into a prime investment paradise and a safe place to hide your cash? The British racing drivers David Coulthard and Jensen Button, who have become permanent residents, spend much of their time driving around the 2.2-square-kilometre mini-nation. The entertainment set, including Roger Moore, Ringo Starr and Shirley Bassey keep a low profile but the big money businessmen are more visible. Philip Green, the extravagant corporate raider, whose three-day birthday in Cyprus cost £5 million, finds Monaco a handy place to meet new economic exiles. But even these flamboyant inhabitants are usually discreet, shunning the nightlife in favour of drinking at the nineteenth century Hotel de Paris, or lunching at Alain Ducasse's three-star restaurant, where £1000 meals are routine.

The big names, though, are far outnumbered by rank-and-file new British expats who belong to what is called the Monaco Mob. These invaders, attracted by the idle display of quickly-acquired wealth, have little to do but walk the dog, sunbathe on the handkerchief-sized beaches, play the fruit machines, read the *Financial Times* or spend the day in France. They may be on the Mediterranean but they settle for recreating a familiar lifestyle in the two pubs, the *Flashman* and the *Ship and Castle*, or visiting nightclubs with English names like *Jimmy'z*.

Unlike other foreigners, few Britons seek Monegasque nationality and few aim to be included in the inner circle around the royal family, who actively discourage too much attention being focused on their tax haven. Monaco, with its non-existent banking laws that have created a zone free of income tax, and capital gains and inheritance taxes, openly encourages investment. This is perfectly legal in a territory where there are no laws on tax fraud even though it has led to a substantial outflow of funds from Britain estimated, according to a confidential report, to be about £1 billion annually. Trying to trace the cash among the 340,000 accounts protected by secrecy laws is impossible, which makes Monaco attractive to those who prefer not to disclose their liquid assets.

Apart from the Britons who have already got a foothold in the principality, there are many more preparing to join them. Under a 1998 law, the Monaco royal family reduced residence qualifications for citizens of European Union nations, making ownership of property unnecessary to obtain a ten-year permit if the applicant has £5 million to invest. Renting a flat and an occasional visit each year is now enough to claim credentials as an honorary Monegasque. These changes, which appear to be having the desired effect of enticing yet more tax avoiders from Britain, are part of a drive to beat Switzerland as Europe's best fiscal hideaway.

So, how will those straining at the leash to prevent the tax authorities from relieving them of some of their precious assets be accommodated, when 300-metre-wide Monaco appears to be bursting at the seams? Well, until recently one-fifth of the mini-state was under water. The royal family has had a massive prefabricated steel segment floated in from Spain to be the base for another residential and business zone. Here, under the watchful eye of the police force and the ubiquitous surveillance cameras, the new British entrepreneurs will have somewhere safe to show off their riches.

34 Monaco is now a principality
    A   dominated by its port.
    B   whose tower blocks appear to be getting taller.
    C   of stark contrasts.
    D   which is spreading in all directions.

35 What does the present influx of Britons into Monaco have in common with that of the nineteenth century?
    A   It is being led by aristocrats.
    B   It is rapid.
    C   It has been caused by the desire to gamble.
    D   It threatens the French domination of Monaco.

36 Most of the rich and famous Britons in Monaco
    A   have been responsible for its post-war transformation.
    B   make numerous new business connections there.
    C   are involved in the entertainment industry.
    D   try to be fairly inconspicuous.

37 The majority of British expatriates in Monaco
    A   live in the same way as they would in Britain.
    B   try to ingratiate themselves with the royal family.
    C   are amongst the worst-behaved inhabitants.
    D   belong to exclusive clubs.

38 What has been the result of the mass exodus of Britons to Monaco?
    A   an investigation by British tax authorities into tax evasion
    B   a freezing of Monegasque bank accounts in British names
    C   a set of new tax laws forbidding transfer of funds out of Britain
    D   a huge reduction in taxes previously paid by expatriates

39 Before 1998, in order to gain a Monaco residence permit, foreigners
    A   were required to spend most of the year in the principality.
    B   had to be from an EU country.
    C   needed to have their own property there.
    D   had to have at least £5 million in a bank account

40 Where will the next group of expatriates be housed?
    A   in the 20% of land yet to be developed
    B   in new blocks that will replace those to be pulled down
    C   in a new housing development near the city centre
    D   in an area of land reclaimed from the sea

Test Five
Paper 2: Writing

Part 1

You must answer this question. Write your answer in **300-350** words in an appropriate style.

1 As part of a project on an English language course, you have been asked to write an essay based on an extract given to you by your teacher. You have been given the extract below. Your essay should include comments on the points raised and your own views on the subject.

> Multi-national companies and governments are quite prepared to spend billions of pounds on advertising and scientific research with a view to making hefty profits and improving the quality of life of a relatively small minority. Yet there are millions of people struggling to survive without adequate food, clean water or educational facilities.

Write your **essay**.

Part 2

Write an answer to one of the questions **2-4** in this part. Write your answer in **300-350** words in an appropriate style.

2 You have read an article in a local newspaper about the changing face of your city. Readers have been invited to send in their opinions concerning new buildings, parks and places of entertainment. Write a letter expressing your views on recent changes and suggesting how any future development should progress.

Write your **letter**.

3 A travel magazine has invited readers to contribute an article to a new section in the next edition entitled *A Great Place to Visit*. Write an article describing a memorable and enjoyable holiday you have had and giving reasons why the place you visited was so special.

Write your **article**.

4 You are employed by a local newspaper. Your editor has asked you to write a review of an exhibition on historical figures from your country. Within your review you should mention one or two people you believe should have been featured in the exhibition but were omitted.

Write your **review**.

Test Five

Hints on writing a review

A review can be about a book, a play or a film but it could also be about some other kind of entertainment or about places to stay on holiday, etc.

In the task outline, you will be told who your target reader is – it could be the readers of a particular kind of magazine, for example. So you need to bear this in mind when you are writing and write in an appropriate register.

Apart from providing information on such things as plot and characters, you will need to include some criticism of what you are describing. This need not all be negative, though.

The review can contain elements of narrative language, as well as description and the language of critics.

As the likelihood of the review being about the media or literature is high, make sure you can use vocabulary relating to these areas well.

You will need to show your review is well-organised. There should be appropriate paragraphing and good linking of the content of the writing. There should be evidence of cohesion when you move from the specific task of reviewing a subject to whatever general question is asked about the subject.

Test Five

Paper 3: Use of English

Hints on how to do Part 5

Comprehension questions
It is essential to read each text through carefully before answering the comprehension questions.

Once you have read the text, you can answer the comprehension questions. When answering, you may use phrases or incomplete sentences. If a question asks 'Why did the captain not want to jump overboard?', you may begin 'Because...'.

Try to answer all the questions and as far as possible use your own words. You will lose marks for 'lifting' straight from the passage, particularly if the question asks you to 'explain in your own words...'. If you have to use vocabulary from the text, then put inverted commas round it so that the examiner can see you know you have used the same words.

You may be required to find words or phrases in the text and put them into your own words. A question may paraphrase or quote a word or phrase from the text and ask you to find synonyms in one of the text. You may be asked to rephrase or interpret a word or phrase or express a key idea from the passage. A question may also test your understanding of something implied but not actually stated.

By the time you have answered the comprehension questions, you should be familiar with the texts. This will make it easier to answer the summary question.

Summary
When writing the summary, bear in mind that you will be writing about both passages, and that you will not be required to write a general summary. Instead, you will have to focus on specific information within the two texts. Consequently, you must be able to distinguish between relevant and irrelevant detail.

Read the question carefully and then underline the points you think are relevant in the texts. There are generally between four and six points from the texts that will need to be summarised, with at least two points from each text. Jot down on a piece of rough paper the points you think are relevant. Look back at the question again. Do your points refer to what you have been asked to do? Have you included all the relevant points?

Remember that you do not need a fully developed introduction that restates the question. It is a summary and you must stick to the point. You do not need to give specific examples to support the points you make. Count your words and make sure you have the required amount (between 50 and 70 words); you will be penalised if your summary is too long. If it is too short, then you have probably missed out information.

The summary is marked out of fourteen marks. Four marks are awarded for content. A maximum of ten marks are awarded for writing a well-constructed paragraph, showing good use of linking words and using your own vocabulary.

Test Five

Part 1

For questions **1-15**, read the text below and think of the word which best fits each space. Use only one word in each space. There is an example at the beginning (**0**).

Example: | **0** | THESE |

Super rich

In (0) ...THESE... days of financial hardship, when the average wage-earner is (1) .... it increasingly difficult to (2) .... by, the results of the first comprehensive survey (3) .... out on the super rich has been published. According to the survey, the number of people in Britain with (4) .... £5 million in ready cash, the minimum amount required to qualify as super rich, (5) .... doubled in the past five years.

Heading this 3,300-strong class is an elite tier of 164 people, (6) .... of whom has at least £100 million in readily accessible assets, including cash, blue-chip shares and bonds. At the (7) .... top of the pile sit eight people with £1 billion (8) .... their name. The report indicates that entrepreneurs selling their businesses, company directors getting bigger pay packets and speculators cashing in (9) .... the property boom have (10) .... rise to the sudden increase in the number of seriously rich citizens.

Datamonitor, the management consultancy that drew (11) .... the report, has revealed that most people in the super-rich class are (12) .... between 55 and 64 and have earned (13) .... than inherited their money. This shows there has been a dramatic shift in wealth (14) .... from those born with a silver spoon in their mouth to people (15) .... businesses are concerned with property, computers and construction.

Part 2

For questions **16-25**, read the text below. Use the word given in capitals at the end of some of the lines to form a word that fits in the space in the same line. There is an example at the beginning (**0**).

Example: | **0** | EXAGGERATION |

About Michelangelo

That Hollywood productions are prone to (0) ...EXAGGERATION... in order to entertain rather than inform is common knowledge, and Charlton Heston's (16) .... of Michelangelo in *The Agony and the Ecstasy* is as guilty of hyperbole as any other star's rendering of a famous artistic figure. This move away from (17) .... is perhaps excusable as it is sanctioned in the name of entertainment, but it does lead to popular (18) ....

EXAGGERATE
PORTRAY

AUTHENTIC

CONCEIVE

There are also certain details omitted that lead to further (19) .... of the image of the central character. In the film mentioned, Michelangelo appeared to be little more than paint-spattered. In reality, though, he was totally (20) .... and it would have been almost impossible to get near him without having to hold one's nose. This was because he was dreadfully (21) .... , seldom bothering to wash or change his socks or boots. When he actually got round to removing these items, several layers of skin came off with them.

DISTORT

REPEL

HYGIENE

Another more important (22) .... from reality concerns his painting the Sistine Chapel ceiling. This feat was accomplished (23) .... from a crouching position with his head tipped back. He did not, as is often thought, do it lying down. Indeed, his (24) .... was so affected by the concentrated effort required that it resulted in a temporary (25) .... to look at drawings unless he held them at arm's length above his head.

DIVERT
METHOD

EYE

ABLE

113

Test Five

Paper 3: Use of English

Part 3

For questions **26-31**, think of one word only which can be used appropriately in all three sentences. Here is an example (**0**)

Example:

0 I'm all for buying stylish shoes, but I draw the .... at spending £500 on a pair.
Could you hold the .... while I check the records, please?
It's a good idea to get out of the firing .... when David and Julie start arguing.

0	LINE

26 It gets quite cold in December but the temperature hardly ever .... below zero.
My birthday .... on a Monday this year, so I think I'll spend a long weekend away in the country.
If Grandpa starts watching TV after 10 o'clock, he invariably .... asleep.

26	

27 Colin doesn't know the first .... about aircraft so why are you going to ask him?
The .... is, how are you going to explain the damage to his car when he gets back?
Feeling very tired, I decided that a few days off work would be the very .... for me.

27	

28 The author goes on to describe the events that follow in .... detail.
Winning the Nobel Peace Prize was a .... achievement for the old statesman.
With its sandy beaches, the resort is .... for sunbathing.

28	

29 Most elderly women prefer to wear .... dresses and skirts rather than those with patterns.
It's quite .... to those who know about environmental matters that global warming will cause widespread flooding in the future.
Although he'd been a .... boy, he grew up to be a handsome man.

29	

30 Being .... as a member of an American street gang normally involves being beaten by existing members.
Since the winner of the Oscar was not at the ceremony, the director .... the award on his behalf.
Martin has never .... that he was wrong to treat Clara that way.

30	

31 When Jackie's father realised she'd taken money from his wallet without asking, he .... into a rage.
Paul must have been in a hurry because he .... past me in the corridor a moment ago.
The time simply .... by while I was on holiday – no sooner had I arrived than it was time to come home.

31	

Test Five

Part 4

For questions **32-39**, complete the second sentence so that it has a similar meaning to the first sentence, using the word given. **Do not change the word given**. You must use between **three** and **eight** words, including the word given. Here is an example (**0**).

Example:

0 I told Mark that scuba diving wasn't for him, but he wouldn't listen.
insisted
Although I told Mark it wasn't for him, ... up scuba diving.

> he insisted on taking

32 Nobody is sure if the project will be allowed to go ahead.
green
It is still uncertain whether the project .... or not.

33 Experts have said the engines did not fail before the aeroplane crashed.
ruled
Engine .... as a possible cause of the air crash.

34 He said that he was annoyed because he wasn't included in the team.
expressed
He .... out of the team.

35 The reason you didn't make money was that you didn't plan the venture properly.
would
Had you .... a profit.

36 I found it very hard to stop smiling when he told me about his mistake.
straight
I had difficulty .... when he told me about his mistake.

37 Being an effective speaker, she is always able to make her audience understand what she means.
message
Because she can speak .... across to her audience.

38 John was absolutely correct in saying that Alice's main problem was her thoughtlessness.
nail
John hit .... said that Alice's thoughtlessness was her main problem.

39 Only three members of the board knew about the merger.
dark
Everybody was .... three members of the board.

Test Five

Paper 3: Use of English

Part 5

For questions **40-44**, read the following texts about thinking. For questions **40-43**, answer with a word or short phrase. You do not need to write complete sentences. For question **44**, write a summary according to the instructions given.

What ongoing daily activity is common to top executives at some of the world's largest corporations such as BT, Siemens, Ericsson and Nokia, four-year-olds in certain schools in Brisbane and Singapore and Khmer villagers? The answer is thinking. But it is not any old thinking: it is parallel thinking, or more specifically the Six Hat thinking framework.

5 Within this framework, which provides a valuable alternative to less constructive traditional methods, thinkers focus their thoughts in one direction at a time. The direction at any point is indicated by the colour of the hat adopted at that moment. For example, the Green Hat requires concentration on the creative aspects related to problem or topic in question. When the Green Hat is in use the primary aim is to produce new ideas or suggest alternatives. When the White Hat is in operation, attention is
10 diverted to gathering all the information relevant to the task in hand.

The Six Hat method is based on a consideration of how chemicals in the brain differ according to the approach taken during the thinking process. Since chemical pre-sensitisation is a key part of brain function and it is not possible to sensitise in all directions at once, it is essential that the different modes of thinking should be separated. Consequently, the vast majority of thinking sessions fail
15 because thinking occurs in several directions at once, which is both unproductive and confusing. After all, when a house needs to be redecorated it is normally done room by room. Another obstacle encountered in traditional thinking is one of ego, where close cooperation is sacrificed in order to retain personal pride. In the Six Hat method, thinking is not a matter of attacking or defending ideas. If someone wants to show off, they can do so by performing well under each hat.

20 Experience has shown that Six Hat thinking is not only much more powerful and effective than argument or discussion but it is also able to reduce meeting times quite spectacularly.

40 What is the writer's purpose in including the list in the question in paragraph 1?
....

41 What effect is created by the use of the phrasal verb 'show off' in line 19?
....

Our traditional emphasis on logic and our dependence on it to solve problems has long been one of the main causes of our lack of effective thinking. Logic, of course, serves a useful purpose, but it is ultimately perception that determines how efficient ordinary thinking is. If the perception is inadequate, no amount of flawless logic will make up for it. Perception is a matter of directing
5   attention. If a person is not looking in the right direction, their intelligence counts for nothing as they will simply not see what they are looking for.

The CoRT (Cognitive Research Trust) programme is designed to correct the faults associated with traditional thinking methods. It is divided into six parts of ten lessons each. The first part deals with broadening perception which involves the introduction of attention-directing tools to eliminate fuzzy
10   and hasty thinking. These tools include: PMI, for a systematic scan of the Plus points, Minus points and Interesting points; OPV, for attention to Other People's Views and C&S, for a deliberate focus on the Consequences and Sequel of a choice or action. The acronyms are necessary in order for the instruction to exist in the mind as an operating concept because mere attitudes have no identity. These astonishingly simple tools are very powerful in their effect, being able to change initial judgements and
15   perception quite radically. The OPV tool, for instance, can break down any barrier created through preconceived ideas that so often prove a limiting factor in traditional thinking methods.

The programme has been in use since 1972 with different cultures, ages and abilities. Its strengths lie in its adaptability, ease of use and ability to avoid those intelligence traps that lead to the poor thinking commonly linked with traditional methods.

42   What exactly does the phrase 'counts for nothing' refer to? (line 5)
....

43   Which two words in the second paragraph reinforce the words 'confusing' and 'obstacle' as applied to traditional thinking in the first text?
....

44   In a paragraph of between **50 and 70** words, summarise **in your own words as far as possible**, the reasons given in the texts as to why traditional thinking methods fail.

....
....
....
....
....
....

Test Five

Paper 4: Listening

Hints on completing the answer sheet

Do not try to complete the answer sheet while you are listening. You have five minutes at the end to transfer your answers from the question paper to the answer sheet. This does not sound long enough, but it is.

Remember that you must use pencil on the answer sheet, not pen. Do not start with Part Two or Three. Start with Part One to ensure that you do not put any answers next to the wrong number.

When you write your answers for the sentence completion, write clearly so that your answer is legible and check your spelling. Do not make your response too long. For the multiple-choices or which person said what, you only need to put A, B, C or D, or the capital letter of the name given. Do not write the whole name and make sure each letter is a capital and easy to read.

Although you have five minutes to complete the answer sheet, you must remain aware of the time as the invigilator will collect both your question paper and answer sheet as soon as the five minutes have elapsed. You cannot ask them to 'wait a minute' as they will not. Finally, if you have time, check that you have transferred your answers without mistakes and have not omitted any answers.

Test Five

Part 1

You will hear four different extracts. For questions 1-8, choose the answer (**A**, **B**, or **C**) which fits best according to what you hear. There are two questions for each extract.

Extract One

You hear a woman talking about oil spills.

1 What does the speaker want scientists to do?
  A   Develop an alternative to oil.
  B   Focus more on dealing effectively with oil spills.
  C   Improve the foam they use.

2 What does she say about the fate of the tortoises?
  A   She can't bear to think about it.
  B   She's sure they'll be fine.
  C   She knows they'll be removed before the oil reaches the coast.

Extract Two

You hear a man talking about cider.

3 What is the significance of the speaker living in Somerset?
  A   It's easy for him to obtain plenty of apples.
  B   The climate is right for cider-making.
  C   It's traditional for people to drink cider there.

4 How does the speaker say cider compares to beer?
  A   It's more popular than beer.
  B   It's just as good to make at home.
  C   It's more difficult to brew.

Extract Three

You hear a man talking about weatherproof clothing.

5 The speaker's yellow cagoule
  A   was only useful when it was misty.
  B   wasn't completely waterproof.
  C   was uncomfortable.

6 What is special about the most recent innovation in weatherproof clothing?
  A   It travels well over rough terrain.
  B   It can alter its heat-retaining or -releasing properties.
  C   It allows water through when necessary.

Extract Four

You hear a woman talking about her garden.

7 What impressed the speaker the most about her new garden?
  A   That it was completed within weeks.
  B   That it contained oak trees.
  C   That it looked like a mature garden.

8 What does the woman think about the price they paid?
  A   It was good value for money.
  B   They paid too much.
  C   The in-laws will think it was cheap.

Test Five

Paper 4: Listening

Part 2

You will hear a radio report about the Maldives. For questions **9-17**, complete the sentences with a word or short phrase.

The [_____ 9] is the location for the 1,100 plus islands that make up the Maldives.

Together with holiday scenery, one finds a [_____ 10] marine and terrestrial environment in the Maldives.

The government's Natural Environment Plans limit the [_____ 11] of the islands' natural resources.

The dangers of [_____ 12] and rising sea level are kept at bay by the sea walls around Malé.

It takes only [_____ 13] to walk across the majority of the islands.

Many of the islands were made when [_____ 14] came up out of the sea and then coral grew around the edge.

Once the islands had developed, with the aid of currents and tides, [_____ and _____ 15] started to grow on them.

Some islands have been eroded so much that they can no longer be seen above [_____ 16].

Providing people [_____ 17] their environment, the Maldive government welcomes tourism.

Part 3

You will hear an interview with two people – Laura Saunders and Hal Vaughan – who work for St Mungo's, the leading London service for homeless people. For questions **18-22**, choose the answer (**A**, **B**, **C** or **D**) which fits best according to what you hear.

18   What happened in 1969?
   A   St Mungo's opened 60 hostels.
   B   St Mungo's was established.
   C   The semi-independent houses were opened.
   D   1,200 people were given shelter.

19   In Britain every night, 1,000 people
   A   stay in semi-independent houses.
   B   ask St Mungo's for help.
   C   sleep on the streets.
   D   stay in specialist homeless accommodation.

20   What is most true amongst the majority of homeless people?
   A   They have problems with their health or with substance abuse.
   B   They are involved in crime.
   C   They are usually under the age of 25.
   D   They have difficult families.

21   St Mungo's believes homeless people should be helped to
   A   understand their problems.
   B   develop their potential.
   C   contact each other.
   D   create their own opportunities.

22   What does Laura say about pets?
   A   They may be the only friend a homeless person has.
   B   They can't be re-housed.
   C   They are no longer allowed in St Mungo's.
   D   They are often in pain.

Part 4

You will hear two people, Tom and Frances, talking about the merits of laptops. For questions **23-28**, decide whether the opinions are expressed by only one of the speakers, or whether the speakers agree.

Write   **T**   for Tom
        F   for Frances
or   **B**   for Both, where they agree.

23   Laptops are useful for people who travel around.

24   I love to be able to e-mail from wherever I am.

25   The laptop offers so much in terms of entertainment.

26   Laptops are a bit expensive.

27   Laptops are a good investment.

28   There ought to be cheap laptops for those who want simpler features.

Test Five — Paper 5: Speaking

Part 1
- Where do you live?
- How you would describe your home area to a foreigner?
- What do you like about your area?
- How do you like to spend your leisure time?
- Are there any leisure activities which don't appeal to you?
- Which major city would you like to visit?
- What do you think are the advantages of living in a city?

Part 2
Here are some pictures depicting people involved in different jobs in the community. (Page 174)

a First I'd like you to look at pictures A and B and talk together about the contribution each person makes to their local community. Discuss which person has the most important role in keeping members of the community happy. You have one minute to do this.

b Now, I'd like you to look at all the pictures. Discuss the emotions or feelings you think might be associated with each job. Then decide which photograph would be the best one for use as the front cover of a local employment magazine featuring community jobs. You have three minutes to talk about this.

Part 3
In this part of the test you are going to talk on your own for about two minutes. You need to listen while your partner is speaking because you'll be asked to comment afterwards.

I'm going to give you a card with a question on it and I'd like you to say what you think. There are some ideas on the card for you to use if you want.

Candidate A, here is your card.

> **Prompt Card A**
>
> The idea of members of the community supporting each other is becoming more difficult to achieve. What are the implications of this?
> - loss of community feeling
> - more crime
> - effect on families

Candidate B, is there anything you don't agree with? (1 minute)
Candidates A and B, how important is it for people to feel part of a community? (1 minute)

Candidate B, look at your card and say what you think.

> **Prompt Card B**
>
> Is the family still as important in modern-day society as it was in the old days?
> - care for young and old
> - role models
> - roots

Candidate A, how does this differ from your experience? (1 minute)
Candidates A and B, what do you think happens in societies where families play a lesser role in people's individual lives? (1 minute)

Both candidates: Now to finish the test, we are going to talk about families and communities. (4 minutes)
- What are the advantages and disadvantages of living in large families?
- What can governments do to support poorer families?
- What do you think of people who argue with or stop speaking to their families?
- Are family members more important than friends?

Test Five

Topics likely to appear

A number of topics have appeared in previous Speaking papers. It's a good idea to keep yourself informed about a variety of topics, so that you have an opinion on them and feel able to have a conversation. Similarly, try to learn vocabulary that relates to topics that might come up, so that you are prepared.

Here are some topics that could appear in the exam:

- The environment
- Fame and success/fortune
- Civilisations and archaeology
- Leadership and dictatorship
- Animals
- Equality (racial, men/women, religious, etc.)
- Human relationships, emotions and feelings
- Sport
- Health and fitness
- Music
- Luck and superstitions
- Technology and progress

Test Six

Paper 1: Reading

Final tips for the exam

Remember that you only have one hour and thirty minutes for the Reading paper, so timing and pacing yourself is very important. You should spend no more than twenty minutes on each part.

Wear a watch to the examination centre and keep an eye on it throughout the exam.

Answer every question. This is, after all, a multiple-choice exam and even by guessing, you stand at least a 25% chance of being correct.

Keeping calm, being familiar with the answer sheet, pacing yourself carefully and having several pencils, a pencil sharpener and an eraser with you will help you feel more relaxed and confident in your approach to this paper.

If you finish early, use the time to check your work. It could mean the difference between passing or failing.

Test Six

Part 1

For questions 1-18, read the three texts below and decide which answer (**A, B, C,** or **D**) best fits each gap.

PRIVATE SCHOOLING

There can be few parents who have not wished they could afford the (1) .... fortune required to send their offspring to a top public school. But when faced with an £18,000-a-year price (2) .... , they have just had to (3) .... their shoulders and accept the situation. These days, however, the astronomical fees need not be an obstacle. With an array of grants and scholarships on offer, from the run-of-the-mill academic awards designed to attract the brain boxes who will help ensure the school's position in the exam league (4) .... to grants rewarding a range of skills, a place at public school can become affordable. As might be expected, there is ferocious competition for places. Candidates must (5) .... their skills in order to reach peak form during the assessment period. This may put pressure on children but it is a small price to pay for the benefits they will (6) .... in the future.

1	A	little	B	slight	C	small	D	slim
2	A	slip	B	label	C	marker	D	tag
3	A	shrug	B	hunch	C	hug	D	stoop
4	A	categories	B	tables	C	divisions	D	catalogues
5	A	take up with	B	beaver away at	C	tie in with	D	brush up on
6	A	harvest	B	gather	C	reap	D	plough

COMMUNICATING WITH BABIES

Because the lack of communication between parents and a baby has often led to feelings of helplessness on the (7) .... of the parents, the introduction of a system of hand (8) .... to overcome the problem has been embraced by some parents. Within this system, six-month-old babies are, for example, taught to signal when they are in pain by putting the (9) .... of their index fingers together.

Sign language has, of course, been taught to deaf infants for years, but it was only when educational psychologists noticed their superior early communication skills that the idea of teaching babies signing (10) .... . Supporters of signing point out that it also allows very young children to express themselves in a basic way. This makes the child less frustrated and therefore less likely to have (11) .... tantrums. Indeed, some proponents have suggested the possibility of more advanced communication, but experts have (12) .... doubt on whether a baby's hand-eye co-ordination would be good enough to achieve this.

7	A	side	B	angle	C	view	D	part
8	A	symbols	B	signs	C	gestures	D	moves
9	A	edges	B	heads	C	points	D	tips
10	A	arose	B	risen	C	ascended	D	raised
11	A	frustration	B	anger	C	temper	D	mood
12	A	shed	B	cast	C	spread	D	inflicted

LYING

Is it best to come clean and tell the truth or lie through your (13) .... when you are in the public (14) .... ? In order to answer this question, it might be useful to look at the worlds of politics and business, where lies are not in short supply.

There are three basic reasons why politicians and company directors, both of whom are adept at lying, choose not to (15) .... the beans. Firstly, they know the truth will not always come out and any potential damage is therefore not inevitable. Secondly, they are also well aware that far from being (16) .... moved by a heart-rending confession of wrongdoing, a discerning public is likely to be as unforgiving as a spurned lover. Thirdly, they have realised that the public has a limited attention (17) .... , which means that stories go away relatively quickly.

The bottom line for these professionals is that even perverting the (18) .... of justice is acceptable if it means saving one's neck. After all, evasion is a life-preserving instinct.

13	A	lips	B	teeth	C	face	D	mouth
14	A	vision	B	eye	C	stare	D	sight
15	A	knock	B	leak	C	drop	D	spill
16	A	utterly	B	completely	C	deeply	D	seriously
17	A	span	B	time	C	spell	D	period
18	A	route	B	path	C	course	D	way

125

Test Six

Paper 1: Reading

Part 2

You are going to read four extracts which are all concerned in some way with holidays. For questions **19-26**, choose the answer (**A**, **B**, **C** or **D**) which you think fits best according to the text.

Tips

To tip or not to tip, that is the question. And it's the one that causes British tourists more moments of embarrassment than almost any other issue. However, a handful of London's top hotels have come up with a cunning solution to spare the blushes. They've started adding a discretionary service charge to guests' bills. Despite the hotels insisting that the charge is optional, it is, in fact, disingenuous. We may find tipping embarrassing, but it's far more embarrassing to stand at a reception desk and demand that the charge should be removed from the bill.

The hotels claim that the charges supplement the income of low-paid back-of-the-house staff who rarely receive tips. Hotel workers are among the lowest-paid in the country with average wages for a room attendant or a porter at a five-star hotel around £5 an hour. Everybody knows that London hotels have been hit hard by the downturn in American visitors, but asking guests to subsidise the low pay of their staff and disguising it as a charge is an underhand way of making more money. What next? A charge for having the sheets on your bed changed?

---

19 The new changes are likely
   A to attract fewer foreign visitors.
   B to increase certain workers' wages substantially.
   C to give porters the salary they truly deserve.
   D to make guests feel even more uncomfortable.

20 The writer regards the move to add the extra charge as
   A clever.
   B dishonest.
   C understandable.
   D fraudulent.

Fun on the slopes

The evening starts with a slow ascent up the slope on the back of a piste machine. As we set off, I realise why there was a rush for seats at the back; my position at the front is exposed to snow thrown up by the machine so that, although I am well wrapped up, the ride is very frosty. But it is a beautiful way to travel to dinner.

After a simple but delicious meal washed down with copious amounts of Savoy wine, I am hurtling down the mountain on a toboggan which is made more difficult to control by the alcohol I have consumed. The couple of dozen people racing down in the dark with me and occasionally crunching into the side of my toboggan are having the same problems, which causes much hilarity as we snake in a wibble-wobble, topsy-turvy fashion down the slope.

It is not as dangerous or stupid as it sounds. The trees are set back far enough from the path for them not to be a problem and I'm sure the slope isn't as steep as it feels. In fact, by the time we reach the end of our twenty-minute ride down the side of this French mountain just outside the main ski resort of Courcheval 1850 in the Alps, the cold wind on our faces has had a sobering effect.

---

21 During the ride down the mountain, the holidaymakers
   A sitting on the front of the toboggans get covered with snow.
   B invariably crash into trees.
   C find colliding with each other amusing.
   D go down the slope as fast as possible.

22 At the end of the toboggan ride the writer
   A is completely exhausted.
   B prepares to ascend the slope again.
   C feels lucky to have got down safely.
   D no longer feels drunk.

A peaceful haven

I was in the mood for Mandu long before I got there. On a slow rail journey across India to this 15th-century ghost city, I changed trains in Lucknow and spent most of a cold, wet, foggy night at this train station. The prospect of Mandu and the peace and quiet of rural India had never seemed more attractive. Mandu, my friends had assured me, was the best place to chill out after Delhi, Agra and Jaipur. But with the remoteness of rural India came the announcement that my train, the Muzaffarpur-Ahmedabad Sabarmati Express would be three hours late. This was a signal for me to swathe myself in my shawl, huddle up on a bench and doze off.

Suddenly, after about ten minutes, I awoke to the sound of strange, wistful music. An audience had gathered around an old man with white hair who stared at me as the piercing flute continued to break the silence. People dropped a few rupees in front of him and eventually he moved on.

Two days later, I was in Mandu, the sort of place where whole days can be set aside for dreaming and hallucinatory flautists are not at all unlikely.

23　The writer went to Mandu because
　　A　he wanted to escape from the hustle and bustle of the city.
　　B　he was interested in supernatural phenomena.
　　C　it was part of the package tour he had booked.
　　D　he had arranged to meet some people he knew there.

24　The old man at Lucknow station
　　A　was also seen by the writer in Mandu.
　　B　disturbed the writer's sleep.
　　C　played requests for passengers on the platform.
　　D　was just a dream.

TARIFA AND TANGIERS

Tarifa, at the southern tip of Andalucia, is both the windiest and most depression-inducing town in Europe. Just as the mistral has a destabilising psychological effect in the south of France, so here the powerful levante can make people fractious. But there may be other factors. Like all border towns, Tarifa suffers from a distinct sense of restlessness, which actively encourages visitors to embark on a day trip to Morocco.

Truman Capote had some useful advice for people intending to make the short crossing to Tangiers. Before coming here you should do three things: be inoculated for typhoid, withdraw your savings from the bank and say goodbye to your friends because Tangiers is a basin that holds you. That was in 1950.

A day in this extraordinary, teeming city with ghosts of William Burroughs and Orson Welles, intolerable hustlers, terrible carpet shops, green-eyed Berbers, fly-blown camels and the ever-present whiff of mature sewage is a wonderful corrective to all the thoughts you had back in Andalucia about the Costa de la Luz being at the end of the world. Now you understand it is simply at the beginning of another one. Few will return to Tarifa from Tangiers without a sense of relief and gratitude. It immediately seems so comfortingly European. And so you realise the redemptive power of travel.

25　What does the writer say about the people of Tarifa?
　　A　They can easily become bad-tempered.
　　B　They frequently pay visits to Tangiers.
　　C　They are insensitive to tourists' needs.
　　D　They are not unlike other Spaniards.

26　Nowadays a trip to Tangiers
　　A　makes people appreciate Truman Capote's advice.
　　B　is a must for bargain hunters.
　　C　is not recommended because of the presence of disease.
　　D　only serves to make Europe more tolerable.

Paper 1: Reading

Part 3

You are going to read an article about shrimp farming. Seven paragraphs have been removed from the article. Choose from the paragraphs **A–H** the one which best fits each gap (**27–33**). There is one extra paragraph which you do not need to use.

Last year the industrialised nations of Europe, North America and Japan peeled, chewed and dribbled their way through over a million tonnes of farmed shrimps worth over £5 billion. Shrimp, it would seem, is absolute pleasure to the taste bud. It is also abundant, protein-rich and readily acceptable to the full range of the world's cuisines. But, as new research by the Environmental Justice Foundation reveals, the true costs of consuming shrimp are dangerously high.

27

The relatively low economic value of this wide variety of marine life compared to that of shrimp mean that it is all discarded. In some shrimp fisheries, by-catch levels of up to 20kg for every 1kg of shrimp have been recorded. The species affected include rare turtles, 150,000 of which are estimated to be caught as by-catch annually.

28

Many of these chemicals are hazardous to human health. The wider environment is also threatened by the release of effluent from shrimp farms into surrounding waters. The effects of shrimp farming can be swift and devastating for coastal communities. Livelihoods that have sustained communities for generations have been disrupted and human rights abuses have been widespread. As a result, a brutal struggle is being waged on the coasts of some of the world's poorest countries, with grassroots campaigners standing up to the giant shrimp-farming industry.

29

Worldwide, opponents of the industry claim that shrimp farming destroys lives and livelihoods of coastal communities and that it causes significant environmental damage. Worldwide, those who have voiced opposition to the industry have been threatened, intimidated, beaten or worse.

30

These sentiments are common to poor, vulnerable and often landless communities that have risen up in protest against shrimp farms. Their anger is principally directed towards the farms blocking access to the coast, reducing local fish catches and destroying mangrove forests that, for generations, have supplied food, medicines, fuel and building materials.

31

For those who do not migrate to cities or overseas, employment must be sought in the very industry that deprived them of their livelihoods in the first place. Shrimp fry are needed to stock the ponds and are harvested directly from the sea. In Bangladesh, women work in the water for eight to ten hours each day. Illness is common. Some collect shrimp fry near the farms, where polluted water causes internal damage and skin diseases. Gloves are not provided and hands begin to rot.

32

Like so many activities that result in resource-use conflict, shrimp farming is destined to continue causing serious health problems that may even be exacerbated unless the industry undergoes radical change. Just as logging and oil exploration has become the focus of international attention following exposure of their adverse effects, so there is an urgent need for scrutiny of the farming methods used to produce this irresistible food.

33

The late Shri Banke Behary Das was a prominent Indian environmental campaigner who exposed the relationship between the people with an insatiable desire for the crustacean and those who worked to satisfy it. In his summary of the situation, he pointed out that the only people who were capable of forcing a change which would improve matters in the industry were the consumers themselves.

A   Father of four, Sebastino Marques de Souza is the latest casualty in this battle. Sebastino was a community activist protesting against the expansion of shrimp farms in the mangrove forests of Brazil. One night, two men – alleged by local campaigner to be connected to the country's burgeoning shrimp-farming industry – approached him under the pretence of needing to buy some petrol and silenced him.

B   Shrimp has traditionally been trawled from the ocean in arguably the most inefficient fisheries practice on the planet. The effect of trawl nets on ecological communities on the ocean floor is the underwater equivalent of clear-cutting forests. Although shrimp trawlers provide only 2% of the world's seafood, they haul in a third of all the global fishing industry's 'by-catch'. In that by-catch over 400 marine species have been identified.

C   In Honduras, violence in the mangroves is no longer a cause of surprise. Even Jorge Varela, director of a local human rights and environmental group has received death threats on numerous occasions. Nevertheless, he has gone on record as saying: 'with the complicity of our government, we have given away our people's patrimony to a few national and foreign individuals, and we have deprived thousands of their livelihoods. We have turned the blood of our people into an appetiser.'

D   Conditions in processing plants also leave much to be desired. Many female workers in Indian shrimp-peeling factories are reportedly held virtual captives by the owners. They may sleep above the processing units where the inhalation of odours and ammonia refrigerants is unavoidable. Common complaints include skin problems and backache from standing for prolonged periods. Handling ice-cold food for long hours has also been linked to arthritis.

E   To the uninitiated, the concept of farming shrimp might seem quite idyllic but the reality's harsh. In fact, shrimp farming is more of an industrial than an agricultural phenomenon. Having been responsible for widespread clearance of productive land and mangrove forests, shrimp farming is also heavily reliant on the use of water pumps, aerators and chemical inputs of pesticides, disinfectants, steroid hormones and antibiotics – including chemicals banned for use in food production by the EU and US.

F   As coastal land has been seized or rendered unusable, hundreds of thousands of rural poor have been displaced. In Ecuador a single hectare of mangrove forest can provide food and livelihoods for ten families but an Ecuadorian shrimp farm of 110 hectares employs just six people during the preparation of shrimp and a further five during the harvest. Likewise, in Sri Lanka's Puttlam district nearly 20,000 lagoon fishers have been obliged to move to the city or flee the country in search of work as shrimp farming has wiped out their traditional livelihoods.

G   Whether stir-fried, barbecued or curried, our passion for this tender crustacean is undeniable. However, to satisfy our appetites, communities worldwide are becoming hungrier, thirstier and less empowered to determine their own lives. This is not a model of development to be proud of.

H   Profits for shrimp-farm owners can be spectacular, and such is the avarice associated with the industry that in some countries politicians and military figures have a vested interest in a shrimp farm. Indeed, there are some who actually have their own farms. This has allowed them to indulge in a lifestyle their countrymen cannot even imagine.

Part 4

You are going to read an article about a seventeenth-century English king. For questions **34-40**, choose the answer (**A**, **B**, **C**, or **D**) which you think fits best according to the text.

A ROYAL DISAPPOINTMENT

For most of his 36 years, the King of Scots, James VI, had dreamed of the day when he could flee his difficult, recalcitrant homeland and ascend the throne of its altogether more sophisticated neighbour. His desire to succeed Elizabeth I had influenced many of his actions, even, said his enemies, the sacrifice of his mother, Mary Queen of Scots, as part of a tacit deal for the English crown. And the desire was far from one-sided. Although enthusiasm was muted by dutiful mourning for Elizabeth, the English also had high expectations. In place of Elizabeth I, whose failure to marry and bear an heir had sparked so many crises, they would now get a family man complete with a Danish wife who had already borne him five children, including an heir, Prince Henry.

But for those inclined to read omens, it was soon easy to see that all was not as it might be. On the day of his coronation, all London turned out to acclaim the King, Queen and Prince Henry. 'The streets seemed to be paved with men,' wrote the poet, Thomas Dekker, 'Stalls instead of rich wares were set out with children. All glass windows were taken down, but in their places sparkled so many eyes that had it not been the day, the light which reflected from them was sufficient to have made one.' But James was no Elizabeth, who had played up to the images the poets had prepared for her, lapped up the crowd's adulation and given them what they wanted. Instead, wrote the 17th-century historian Arthur Wilson, James 'endured the day's brunt with patience, being assured he should never have another.' It was a sign of things to come.

It was soon clear that James's natural disposition led him away not only from crowds but from what many regarded as his kingly duties, ideas about which James drew directly on his experience as King of Scots. Seeing himself as the incarceration of the Law, he would have no truck with England's Common Law. Disastrously, James regarded parliament as 'nothing but the King's great council,' advising his son to 'hold no Parliaments, but for necessity of new laws, which would be but seldom.' In Scotland he had demanded that all proposals for laws should be submitted to him 20 days before the opening of Parliament so he could select those he wanted. No other legislation would be debated, and even laws passed by Parliament would only become statutes with his final approval – 'and if there be anything that I dislike, they raze it out before.' But to the English Parliament, a sturdy body with a developed sense of its corporate influence, such views were loathed. James was to wage a war of attrition against Parliament – and lose.

Indeed, James was strangely aloof from many of the phenomena we would now recognise as peculiarly Jacobean. England had entered the 17th century with immense promise. A new world was opening up for English adventurers and merchants, with exciting and exotic new territories from Virginia to Goa. Modern science and medicine were being born through the insights of Francis Bacon and William Harvey, both of whom were personal servants of the king. English theatre was at its legendary peak, with Shakespeare himself one of James's own acting troupe, the King's Men. Inigo Jones brought the latest continental taste to the King's Banqueting House in Whitehall and to his masques at court. But James seemed unimpressed. He mocked colonial exploration, fell asleep during England's most celebrated plays and showed little interest in scientific advances.

Perhaps the most disastrous of his shortcomings was highlighted during a visit to Beauvoir, where he displayed a preference for watching little boys fighting. He could neither stand seeing soldiers in battle nor watching men being drilled. James himself admitted to his 'fearful nature'. This was the man who had survived not only the Gunpowder Plot of 1605 but also the 'Gowrie Conspiracy' of 1600. He had also seen the corpse of his assassinated grandfather at the age of five. He attributed his fears to the murder of his mother's secretary David Riccio by his father's supporters while Mary was pregnant with him. As he proclaimed to the English parliament in 1605, James had been the victim of 'daily tempests of innumerable dangers, not only since my birth but even as I justly say before my birth.' Here, at least in his own analysis, were planted the true roots of James's apparent disregard for the grind of English government: not a deliberate laziness or whimsical superiority, but a fear of conflict. But it was precisely in conflict – with his parliament, his ministers, his lawyers, his favourites and his children – that James was to spend his reign.

34 How did James compare England to Scotland?
  A He thought it would be easier to rule.
  B He believed it was strategically more important.
  C He believed its people were less responsible.
  D He suspected it had more potential for trade.

35 How did the English react to James's desire to rule England?
  A They welcomed it.
  B They reluctantly accepted it.
  C They found it inexplicable.
  D They thought it was suspicious.

36 How did James react on the day of his coronation?
  A He was astonished by the turnout.
  B He realised he would have to develop a new image.
  C He concealed his true feelings.
  D He regretted his decision to become monarch.

37 What was James's connection with the English legal system?
  A He refused to have anything to do with it.
  B He saw himself as its founder.
  C He alone made new laws.
  D He was the only person who could appoint judges.

38 What was England like at the time of James's ascent to the throne?
  A There were curious developments taking place.
  B It was a fashionable place to live.
  C Medical facilities had greatly improved.
  D It provided a range of new opportunities.

39 James distanced himself from the daily affairs of state because
  A of his fear of failure.
  B he disliked confrontation.
  C he was easily bored by ministers.
  D he believed such duties were beneath him.

40 How could the problems James encountered in his relationships best be described?
  A didactic
  B ironic
  C superficial
  D complex

Test Six — Paper 2: Writing

Part 1

You must answer this question. Write your answer in **300-350** words in an appropriate style.

1. You work for the town council of a popular seaside resort. Many locals have made complaints about the tourists and the effects they have on their lives during the summer. You have been asked to investigate and write a proposal on how to deal with the problems highlighted in the extracts below which you have been given.

> Tourism in our seaside town is all very well, but tourists make so much noise at night that it is difficult to get to sleep. They also leave rubbish everywhere and generally spoil the place. I say enough is enough!

> As a pensioner, I find that the increase in prices during the tourist season causes me financial problems. Very often I have to do my shopping elsewhere.

> I realise that tourists bring in much-needed cash, but the inconvenience we locals have to suffer is simply not worth it. More facilities are desperately needed so that we can go out without having to wait in long queues and traffic jams or be pushed around by tourists.

Write your **proposal**.

Part 2

Write an answer to one of the questions **2-4** in this part. Write your answer in **300-350** words in an appropriate style.

2. After receiving a number of letters about how difficult it is to meet people after moving to a new location, a young people's magazine has invited readers to contribute an article to a special section entitled *Making New Friends*. Write an article describing ways of meeting people in a new environment and giving ideas on how to develop relationships.

   Write your **article**.

3. You work for a TV channel which is thinking of broadcasting a new reality show. Your manager has asked you to write a report about a very popular reality show, including comments made by viewers and how it could be improved.

   Write your **report**.

4. You are employed by a local council. You have recently been involved in the building of a new arts centre which includes a cinema complex, theatre, art gallery, exhibition centre, cafés and a restaurant. A few letters criticising the centre have been published in a recent edition of the local newspaper. In your opinion, the letters are both unfair and incorrect. Write a letter to the editor commenting on the letters and defending your point of view.

   Write your **letter**.

Test Six

Hints on how to answer the set book question

Reading one of the set books gives you the advantage of a further choice in the **Writing** paper. You also have the pleasure of reading something in English, other than a course book.

It is essential that you know the book well. One quick reading of it is not enough. An in-depth knowledge is required to prove you know and understand the book's plot and its characters. As you read the book, make notes about what happens in each chapter. This will help you to revise for the exam without having to reread the entire book. You should also write a description of each character and note down how the plot develops. Practise writing essays on the book too to really 'immerse' yourself in it.

The exam question could ask you to write about:

- the characters and their relationship with each other: whether they like one another, how they affect one another, what they say about another person, etc.
- the plot, particularly the scenes important to understanding the whole book
- the theme (in other words, what the book is about)
- any sub-plot
- the setting (where, and sometimes when, the story takes place)

The exam question could also contain a quotation that relates to a character and it might ask you to comment on how true the quotation is about the person or what effect it has on someone else in the story.

Try not to approach the book as just another book to plough through to pass the exam. Read and enjoy it. English is not all grammar, vocabulary and examinations!

One last reminder
If you do not like the set book question that appears the day you take the exam, do not answer it. You may have read the book but this does not mean you have to choose to write a composition about it.

Final tips for the exam

On the day of the exam you will be given the question paper and some sheets of paper on which you can plan, make notes and write your composition. Put one line through your notes or plan so that the examiner knows not to mark it and if you need more paper, put your hand up and ask. You must hand all the pieces of paper in when you have finished.

Remember to write the number of the question you are answering clearly on the answer sheet and remember that you must write in blue or black ink. White correcting fluid is not allowed. Make sure your writing is easy to read and set out in clearly arranged paragraphs.

You have two hours to complete two compositions. Read the questions carefully, decide which one in Part 2 you are going to write and make sure you understand what you have to do. Watch the time. Do not spend too long on the first essay, or you will find that you have to rush the second.

Try to plan your work so that you can answer the question fully. Do not forget to check that you have actually answered the question.

Check:

- your spelling
- verb/subject agreement
- use of *this*/*these*
- your use of tenses
- word order
- your range and variety of vocabulary
- the amount of words you have written
- that you have used paragraphs
- your punctuation

You will not be given extra time to write a neater version.

Test Six

Paper 3: Use of English

Final tips for the exam

Always bear in mind that you are answering onto a separate answer sheet in pencil and as the examiner needs to be able to read your answers, ensure that everything you write is readable and clear. If you change your mind, make sure you erase your first answer completely before writing the new one.

In Part 1, read the gap-filling cloze passage through carefully before you write any words in. If you get stuck on one or two gaps, leave it for a while and go on to another exercise but do not forget to come back to it. Attempt every gap. Only put one word in each gap. Read through the whole text again when you have finished to see that what you have put in makes sense at paragraph and text level, rather than just at sentence level. You have plenty of time to do this, so do not think it does not matter, as it does. This rechecking could mean the difference between passing and failing!

In Part 2, don't forget that you may have to make more than one change to a word. For example, you may be given the word *understand* and be expected to come up with *misunderstandings*.

In Part 3, remember that the missing word must be the same part of speech in each of the three sentences. Make sure the word is correct for all three sentences.

When you are transforming a sentence in Part 4, don't forget that there are usually two changes that need to be made to the sentence. You may be required to change the sentence from active to passive, or to make a personal construction impersonal or a positive construction negative.

With Part 5, read the passages carefully and do not try to do the summary before you have answered the comprehension questions. Attempt every question. Count the words when you have completed the summary.

It is important to check all your answers and take your time.

Test Six

Part 1

For questions **1-15**, read the text below and think of the word which best fits each space. Use only one word in each space. There is an example at the beginning (**0**).

Example: | **0** | UNTIL |

Preservation by multiplication

It was not (0) ......UNTIL...... the 17th century that the idea of preserving the past was adopted. Of course, preservation seems a good idea, but it is (1) .... that may be doomed since pollution, insects or rust eventually destroy artefacts, no (2) .... how many protective measures are (3) .... The Sphinx is a case (4) .... point. Although it has so far survived the ravages of time, its current problems are no (5) .... urgent. Cairo's suburban sprawl has now extended almost as (6) .... as the Sphinx, (7) .... enigmatic gaze now rests on a Pizza Hut and a Kentucky Fried Chicken, a sign that pollution around the monument is at its (8) .... level ever.

Since nothing can be done to prevent so-called progress, efforts to preserve historical objects appear to be coming up (9) .... even more problems. And the solution may involve a change in attitude (10) .... than new methods of preservation. Instead of (11) .... attempts to freeze time by doing everything (12) .... to keep originals intact, another ploy with a peculiarly Eastern philosophy could be adopted. (13) .... westerners, the Chinese do not believe that copies are inferior (14) .... originals, so painstakingly constructed copies are readily accepted. Such a (15) .... of view may be difficult to understand but it would, if nothing else, almost eliminate crimes involving antiquities.

Part 2

For questions **16-25**, read the text below. Use the word given in capitals at the end of some of the lines to form a word that fits in the space in the same line. There is an example at the beginning (**0**).

Example: | **0** | HISTORICAL |

A successful failure

If there is one (0) ......HISTORICAL..... figure that has been regarded as a	HISTORY
(16) .... during his lifetime by so many biographers and yet is	FAIL
remembered by secondary school history students as a (17)	LEGEND
explorer and campaigner, it is David Livingstone.	
As an explorer, he erred (18) .... in thinking that that the Zambezi river was	DISASTER
navigable and he misidentified the source of the Nile. In addition, by the time	
he died, his campaign against the East African slave trade had had (19)	DISAPPOINT
little success. He was not much better as a husband or father, either, leaving his family	
behind for years as he trampled thousands of miles over inhospitable rugged African terrain.	
Despite his mistakes and the fact that his (20) .... was often less than	BEHAVE
(21) .... , he deserved more recognition than he has been given by	EXAMPLE
experts. Indeed, there were values he (22) .... that have held him in high	BODY
esteem in some circles. He found the (23) .... of the blacks ensnared in the	TREAT
booming African slave trade so distasteful that he fought (24) .... to stamp	TIRE
it out. His attempts may have failed during his active campaign but in the year after his death,	
the Sultan of Zanzibar signed a treaty with Britain guaranteeing the (25) .... of	ABOLISH
the East African slave trade, an agreement Livingstone had dreamed of.	

Test Six — Paper 3: Use of English

Part 3

For questions **26-31**, think of one word only which can be used appropriately in all three sentences. Here is an example (**0**).

Example:

0   If you don't pull your ...., everybody else will have more work to do.
Your agreeing to lend me the money I need is really a .... off my mind.
Fashion models have to watch their ...., otherwise they don't get booked for shows.

| 0 | WEIGHT |

26   All the children were in .... spirits after they had been told about the trip to the zoo.
After winning the lottery, Margaret was determined to live the .... life and indulge her every whim.
There's no need for you to adopt that .... and mighty attitude with me.

| 26 | |

27   Henry's publishing company has not yet decided exactly when to .... his next novel.
Remember to .... the handbrake properly before you drive off.
If there is new evidence that proves his innocence, it is likely that the authorities will .... him from jail.

| 27 | |

28   Talks between the two leaders .... when they were unable to reach agreement on a peace plan.
The football manager was under so much stress that he .... during a game and had to be taken to hospital.
So many people were dancing at the party that the floor .... beneath them.

| 28 | |

29   Farmers have been .... hard by the recent bad weather and will probably face financial problems next year.
The driver in front of me almost .... a pedestrian crossing the road.
Share prices .... an all-time low yesterday as they plunged by 3.2%.

| 29 | |

30   Unfortunately, Janice took the road that .... to the coast and ended up in the wrong village.
The silver medallist .... the race until the last few metres when he was overtaken by his great rival.
Norma .... a quiet life in the country after escaping from the hustle and bustle of the city.

| 30 | |

31   The road sign in the shape of an inverted triangle means you must give .... to traffic on the main road.
Elizabeth's father can't refuse her anything so she always gets her own ....
I don't want you to give me any money for expenses; I prefer to pay my own ....

| 31 | |

Part 4

For questions **32-39**, complete the second sentence so that it has a similar meaning to the first sentence, using the word given. **Do not change the word given**. You must use between **three** and **eight** words, including the word given. Here is an example (**0**).

Example:

0 Her sole purpose in life was to give her children the best possible education.
   committed
   She .... her children the best possible education.

   | was committed to giving |

32 Mrs Jackson's condition improved dramatically when she was treated in a revolutionary new way.
   led
   A revolutionary new .... Mrs Jackson's condition.

33 She didn't realise he had been murdered until she saw the body.
   dawn
   Only when .... her that he had been murdered.

34 While she was on safari, she only just managed to escape from a charging rhino.
   skin
   It was only by .... in escaping from a charging rhino while she was on safari.

35 Would financial problems mean having to abandon your research?
   come
   Were you .... you have to abandon your research?

36 The goalkeeper was criticised more heavily than anyone else for the team's defeat.
   brunt
   The goalkeeper .... levelled at the team for its defeat.

37 Unless the partners could raise enough capital, their business would be unsuccessful.
   hinged
   The success of the partners' business .... enough capital.

38 The spokesperson did not want to give any specific information about the cause of the fire.
   prepared
   The spokesperson .... detail about the cause of the fire.

39 She didn't try to improve her marks until last term.
   made
   It wasn't until .... to improve her marks.

Test Six

Paper 3: Use of English

Part 5

For questions **40-44**, read the following texts on telepathy. For questions **40-43**, answer with a word or short phrase. You do not need to write complete sentences. For question **44**, write a summary according to the instructions given.

The direct transference of thought from one person to another without using the usual sensory channels of communication is known as telepathy. While its existence has not yet been proved, the respect it has gained is a far cry from the days when it was thought to exist only in the realms of fantasy. A number of serious studies of the phenomenon have been carried out by reputable institutions, which has given it credibility in
5 many scientific circles.

Telepathic abilities are believed to be closely related to one person (the receiver) being able to read the thoughts of another person (the sender). The way in which this occurs is rather like tuning into a radio station. In both cases the key is to find the right frequency so that a communication link can be established.

Although telepathy can be developed through meditation techniques and used at will, the vast majority are
10 unable to engage in thought transference. This, however, has not always been true. According to some researchers, telepathy was once essential for the survival of primitive species but over the course of time has largely been lost or made redundant. Nevertheless, there are circumstances in which telepathy is more likely to surface naturally. Twins, for example, are able to communicate in this way far more readily than regular siblings who, in turn, exhibit greater telepathic skills than people from different families. Those
15 among us who are learning-challenged also possess greater potential for telepathic communication. Their inability to connect naturally with others forces them to adopt 'higher senses' in order to do so.

40 In the first paragraph, how does the writer view the way telepathy is regarded nowadays?
   ....

41 Explain in your own words why the writer has chosen to use the expression 'made redundant'. (line 12)
   ....

The word 'telepathy' is derived from the Greek terms 'tele' and 'pathos' which mean 'distant' and 'feeling'. The term was coined as far back as 1882 by the French psychical researcher Frederic H Meyers.

Since then, the phenomenon has made great strides both in its struggle for acceptance and its understanding. Experiments conducted in the field have revealed that telepathy most often occurs in incidents of crisis where a relative or close friend is experiencing great difficulties or has been involved in an accident. The information transmitted in such cases seems to arrive in different forms like thought fragments received in dreams, visions, mental images, or words that pop into the mind. Often such information causes the receiver to change travel plans or a daily schedule. This ability to make use of telepathy appears to be related to the emotional state of the parties involved, irrespective of the distance or obstacles between them. Telepathy can also be induced in the dream state, in which blood volume changes during the sending phase and the brain waves of the recipient change to match those of the sender.

Even though various theories have been advanced to describe the way telepathy functions, its mechanism is as elusive as its systematic testing is arduous. Since the success of testing would appear to be heavily dependent on one's emotional state, replicating results is fraught with difficulty.

42 What does the expression 'pop into' in line 7 suggest about telepathy?

43 Which phrase in paragraph 2 reinforces the way in which telepathy is thought to work as described in the first text?

44 In a paragraph of between **50 and 70** words, summarise **in your own words as far as possible**, the factors mentioned in the texts which make telepathic communication more likely.

Paper 4: Listening

Final tips for the exam

Most of these tips repeat the earlier advice throughout this book but read them again for revision.

Try to

- read every question in each part before you hear the cassette for the first time.
- use this information to imagine what you are going to hear.
- keep listening, even if there is a word you do not understand.
- answer as many questions as you can the first time you listen.
- check your answers and complete anything you have missed the second time you hear the tape.

Try not to

- lose your concentration.
- worry about understanding every word.
- spend so much time writing the answers to the sentence completion that you forget to listen to the next part.
- worry if you don't catch everything the first time you listen.
- be distracted by the wrong answers in the multiple-choice questions. Focus more on the questions first.

The answer sheet

- Do not try to complete the answer sheet before the end of the test.
- Remember to use a pencil on the answer sheet.
- Make sure you start at number one on the answer sheet and work through it in sequence.
- If you have time, check your answers on the answer sheet.
- Check your spelling and that the answer is grammatically correct.

Test Six

Part 1

You will hear four different extracts. For questions **1-8**, choose the answer (**A**, **B**, or **C**) which fits best according to what you hear. There are two questions for each extract.

Extract One

You hear a woman talking about skiing.

1 The woman lives
   A a long way from the indoor ski slope.
   B not far from the indoor ski slope.
   C in a different country from the indoor ski slope.

2 The temperature of what is minus two?
   A the water
   B the snow
   C the air

Extract Two

You will hear a boss speaking to a member of his staff.

3 The boss is not unhappy about
   A the quality of Shirley's work.
   B Shirley's timekeeping.
   C the way Shirley dresses.

4 Shirley's contract enables the boss
   A to reduce Shirley's income immediately.
   B to sack Shirley straight away.
   C to change working conditions without notice.

Extract Three

You hear a woman talking about her job in a museum.

5 How do people usually appear when the speaker tells them what her job is.
   A fascinated
   B bored
   C intimidated

6 Why does the speaker liaise with similar museums overseas?
   A To arrange for them to lend her museum some exhibits.
   B To compare exhibits.
   C To acquire more permanent pieces.

Extract Four

You hear a man talking about photography.

7 Why does the speaker find photographing birds more difficult than photographing other wildlife?
   A They are harder to catch than other wildlife.
   B Any noise will make the birds fly away.
   C There are fewer birds than other animals.

8 Why does the speaker complain about being in the hide-out?
   A It gives him cramp.
   B There isn't a lot of room.
   C It makes it more difficult to get the perfect shot.

Test Six

Paper 4: Listening

Part 2

You will hear a radio report about forensic evidence. For questions **9-17**, complete the sentences with a word or short phrase.

At _____[9], one can often find various tool marks.

Tools used in a crime often leave behind _____[10] marks.

The marks left after a crime are influenced by the tool used, the _____[11] of the surfaces and the force used.

Pressure applied to two sides of an object will leave _____[12] marks.

Finding the tool near to where the crime occurred will give forensic scientists _____[13] about who committed the crime.

Footwear marks can provide evidence because they can be _____[14]

Footwear marks can show _____[15] of events that took place during the crime.

If there is snow on the ground, _____[16] footprints are left.

Forensic experts can often tell the precise _____ and _____[17] of a shoe as well as the size.

Test Six

Part 3

You will hear an interview with Carol Lyons, an aromatherapist, who has established herself as something of an authority in this field of alternative therapy. For questions **18-22**, choose the answer (**A, B, C** or **D**) which fits best according to what you hear.

18 What are essential oils?
    A   spices extracted from plants
    B   oils essential for the growth of the plant
    C   fragrant oils
    D   plant oils

19 What does Carol think is most interesting about massage?
    A   that Hippocrates used it
    B   that it's old and simple
    C   that it can both energise and relax
    D   that it's soothing

20 Aromatherapy massage depends on
    A   understanding between the therapist and the patient.
    B   feelings of comfort and well-being.
    C   deciding which oils to administer.
    D   unique massage techniques.

21 What is the basis for deciding which blend of oil to use?
    A   the patient's preferences and wishes
    B   the questions the patient asks
    C   the patient's needs and the aim of the massage
    D   what the therapist wants to achieve

22 What will qualified therapists advise on?
    A   how to blend oils
    B   the safety aspects of aromatherapy
    C   the dilution of oils
    D   pharmaceutical remedies

Part 4

You will hear two people, Jasper and May, talking about a film they have recently seen and are both reviewing. For questions **23-28**, decide whether the opinions are expressed by only one of the speakers, or whether the speakers agree.

Write   **J**   for Jasper
            M   for May
or   **B**   for Both, where they agree.

23 The film didn't portray the same story as the book.

24 I watch films without comparing them to the book.

25 It was hard to distinguish between fact and fantasy.

26 The digitally-produced effects were superb.

27 The male lead wasn't well cast.

28 The female lead is likely to go on to be more successful.

Test Six
Paper 5: Speaking

Part 1

- What are your hobbies and interests?
- How much of your free time do you spend with your family?
- How much time do your studies or work take up each week?
- What's your idea of a perfect holiday?
- Do you plan to travel more in the future?
- What is your motivation for learning English?
- How will you keep up your level of English once you stop studying?

Part 2

Here are some pictures related to various health issues. (Page 175)

a First look at pictures A and B and talk together about how the people might be feeling. You have about one minute to do this.

b Now, I'd like you to look at all the pictures. I'd like you to imagine that a pressure group is organising a campaign called *Prevention is better than cure*.

Talk together about the issues suggested in each of these pictures and decide which three the campaign should concentrate on. You have three minutes to talk about this.

Part 3

In this part of the test you are going to talk on your own for about two minutes. You need to listen while your partner is speaking because you'll be asked to comment afterwards.

I'm going to give you a card with a question on it and I'd like you to say what you think. There are some ideas on the card for you to use if you want.

Candidate A, here is your card.

Prompt Card A

What are the implications of the increasing percentage of elderly people in our population?
- care
- financial support
- changing work and leisure

Candidate B, what do you think?
Candidates A and B, is it right that researchers are constantly trying to find ways of prolonging life?

Candidate B, look at your card and say what you think.

Prompt Card B

What are the implications of human cloning?
- choosing members of society
- ethical dilemmas
- costs

Candidate A, is there anything you would like to add?
Candidates A and B, can you think of any positive aspects to human cloning?

Both candidates: Now to finish the test, we're going to talk about technological advances.

- Are there any areas where technological development ought to be more strictly controlled?
- How do you feel about people having their bodies preserved in ice after their death (in the hope that they can be brought back to life in the future)?
- What other technological achievements do you envisage in the future?
- Why do some people feel afraid of computers and new technology?

Final tips for the exam

Approach this part of the exam in a relaxed manner. Students sometimes become so anxious about the interview that it hinders their speech and they do badly in something that they normally excel in. The interviewers are there to help you and are generally very friendly.

Do not prepare any sort of 'speech' before you have the interview. The examiner will know because it will not sound natural. Be yourself, smile and try to relax.

For the first few minutes you will be talking about yourself. Most people like doing this and it's not difficult. Try to be imaginative and if the interviewer asks you what you do in your spare time, do not just say 'I do not have any spare time or hobbies'. You might say 'If I had the time, I would like to collect masks'. You could talk about a hobby or pastime you used to do or would like to do. You can even just pretend you have a hobby. The examiner is there to test your ability to speak English, not your general knowledge, your point of view or whether you are telling the truth or not. They will not come back in five years to find out if you really have become a doctor!

When you speak about the photograph(s), do not just describe them or it, but say how the photo makes you feel or make some comment about the place, etc. Do not ask the examiner to change the topic or say that you do not know anything about it. Try and talk about the subject even if you genuinely do not know much about it. Move the conversation on and try to bring it round to something you can talk about.

In this part of the exam, you will have to spend much of the time speaking to another candidate. This candidate may or may not have a good level of English. You need to prepare yourself for either situation and the only way to do this is to practise speaking to different members of your class in English. When you have to do pairwork in class, don't always sit next to your best friend. Make sure you can deal with having a discussion with someone who doesn't respond much or with someone who talks too much!

Above all, be friendly, smile and relax. The interviewer is human and if he/she enjoys the interview, it is only human to give a better mark. Remember how many interviews they conduct in a day – try to make yours that little bit different.

Test One

Test your vocabulary

Study the vocabulary used in **Practice Test 1** and then try the exercises below.

A The right word

Complete each blank with the correct form of a word from the boxes. You may use a word more than once.

| risk | wind | fear | bandwagon | leaf |

1. Eager for success, Dawn jumped on the .... and opened an Internet café.
2. Although I've been on many safaris, I've never been at .... from a wild animal.
3. As soon as Serena's friends got .... of the rumour that she'd won the lottery, they contacted her.
4. If you don't turn over a new .... , you'll find yourself without a job.
5. He didn't tell her what he really thought for .... of insulting her.

| reap | come | gather | capture | run | shed | hold | go |

6. Despite his age, Mark is still able to .... his own in a tennis match with Bob.
7. After years of financial difficulties, Tina is finally .... the rewards of all her hard work.
8. It .... without saying that you're expected to be at the exam on time.
9. Because the investigation failed to .... light on the matter, nothing of any importance .... back to me.
10. The police spent the entire weekend trying to .... enough evidence to make an arrest.
11. If a film doesn't have enough action, it will never .... my imagination.
12. Knowing that the children would .... riot if they were left alone, she decided to give the party a miss.

| short | full | odd | tidy | wide |

13. They started the business in the hope of making a .... sum in a .... space of time.
14. The idea that you're ready to compete after only two weeks of practice is nothing .... of ridiculous.
15. Tourists come from far and .... to ski in the Alps in winter.
16. Although I'm not that keen on exercise, I do like going out for the .... walk through the countryside.
17. I was tested to the .... extent of my abilities.

| positively | remotely | fully | simply |

18. The police questioned everyone even .... connected to the firm.
19. I felt .... humiliated by what the director said about me.
20. I'm .... aware that you're unhappy with things, but there's nothing I can do about it.
21. It's .... a matter of time before he finds out the truth.

146

Test One

B Words in use

Use the words and phrases on the left to complete the sentences on the right. Make sure the word or phrase is in the correct form.

1
- in line with
- in terms of
- by means of
- in keeping with

a .... action, the film was rather disappointing.
b She reached the top of her profession .... hard work and little else.
c All salary increases this year will be 2-9%, ... inflation.
d .... tradition, he asked her father's permission to marry her.

2
- barely
- remotely
- virtually
- roughly

a I am not even .... interested in computers.
b As my father is .... bankrupt, I have to help him out financially.
c The population of Great Britain is .... 55 million.
d They were so remarkably similar that I was .... able to tell them apart.

3
- complete
- total
- full
- whole

a Did you know that a fully-grown python can swallow a pig .... ?
b There was a .... eclipse of the sun in 1999.
c The lawyer promised to prosecute the criminals to the .... extent of the law.
d Make sure that the pack of cards is .... before you start playing.

4
- prime
- lead
- top
- average

a He was a(n) .... student so we were surprised when he was accepted by Oxford University.
b Who played the .... role in the first James Bond film?
c After being identified in a line-up, he became a .... suspect in the murder investigation.
d Only if he is in .... form will George beat Mike in the final.

5
- fight
- battle
- stand
- conflict

a He took a .... on the question of the proposed dismissal and refused to support it.
b Their grandfather was killed in .... during the Second World War.
c She dislikes .... of any kind and does her best to avoid it.
d He'll put up a .... if he feels threatened.

Test One — Test your vocabulary

C Phrasal verbs
Match the phrasal verbs in bold with their definitions.

1 You'd better **brush up on** your French before you go to Paris. ....
2 What did the children **get up to** while you were shopping? ....
3 They **squared up to** each other, ready to resolve their differences through violence. ....
4 Manufacturers often **cash in on** the popularity of TV characters. ....
5 Geoff has been **passed over** for the position of sales manager. ....
6 Being proud of her athletic ability, she seldom **shies away from** a challenge. ....
7 The footballer didn't **live up to** the promise he'd shown as a teenager. ....
8 Despite the rain, our weekend away **turned out to be** highly enjoyable. ....
9 How would you **set about** organising a conference for 200 people? ....
10 I'd been told the service was excellent and the staff didn't **let me down**. ....

a	do something naughty	f	be frightened of
b	disregard	g	get in a position ready to fight
c	be the result in the end	h	begin to do
d	disappoint	i	regain one's skill
e	fulfil one's potential	j	make money by taking advantage of

D Preposition practice
Use the prepositions below to complete the sentences which follow. Some prepositions are used more than once.

on   to   in   by   from   out of   towards   at

1 I would only do a job I disliked .... of necessity.
2 With all her flights of fancy, Karen seems to be losing her grip .... reality.
3 If there were an alternative .... working twelve hours a day, I would take it.
4 Unable to contact the manager .... phone, I sent her a fax.
5 Any breakages you are responsible for will be deducted .... your wages.
6 Feeling trapped in a small village, Fiona moved to the capital .... pursuit of fame.
7 The majority of shareholders voted .... favour of a merger.
8 He felt very sympathetic .... his sister after her husband had been lost .... sea.
9 We can only deal with complaints submitted .... writing.
10 It's highly likely that the team's star player will be transferred .... a top European club.

148

E Word building

Use the words in capitals at the end of each sentence to form a word that fits in the space in the same sentence.

1 It is usually the .... of an idea that makes it successful. SIMPLE
2 Finding the lure of Hollywood .... , Jane packed her bags and left for America. RESIST
3 Being surrounded by hostile nations often forces a country to seek a military .... with an unlikely 'friend'. ALLY
4 People living in areas of high air pollution often suffer from .... problems. RESPIRE
5 It must be totally .... to live in poverty without the hope of an improvement in one's standard of living. MORALE
6 Working in a luxury hotel gave me an .... into how the rich and famous behave. SEE
7 He wanted to .... that he would catch the train, so he arrived at the station an hour early. SURE
8 The more frequently you use a computer, the more .... it becomes. DISPENSE

F Tricky pairs

Compare each sentence by choosing the correct word.

1 Interest *rates/proportions* used to be a lot higher than they are now.
2 It's a *foreseen/foregone* conclusion that science will progress at an ever-increasing pace.
3 The biologist's search for the leap frog was fruitless because the creature proved to be *highly/deeply* elusive.
4 She didn't want to tell the truth for *fear/danger* of getting into trouble.
5 What we saw during the war *surpassed/extended* all description.
6 The *prevailing/dominant* member of a herd of deer is always the strongest.

Test Two

Test your vocabulary

Study the vocabulary used in **Practice Test 2** and then try the exercises below.

A The right word

Complete each blank with the correct form of a word from the boxes. You may use a word more than once.

| previous | advance | beforehand | prior |

1 I distinctly remember you telling me .... to the meeting that you would support me.
2 Her .... novel involved so many twists and turns that I could make neither head nor tail of it.
3 If Carlos had been told .... that he would be the only one to sing in the show, he would never have agreed to do it.
4 I wish I knew the exam questions in ....

| thorny | deadly | fierce | rival |

5 To be perfectly honest with you, I doubt whether the company can survive in the face of such .... competition.
6 There are many .... diseases in that country so you'd better get inoculated before you go.
7 Who's at fault is a .... question as they're both to blame, but won't admit it.
8 If he had been told he would be on a .... gang's turf, he would never have gone alone.

| fend | count | bridge | stand | maintain | give | pose |

9 When I visited her, she .... me the impression that she could .... for herself despite her disability.
10 We .... to make a healthy profit if the firm can .... its current growth rate.
11 You can .... yourself lucky that street crime doesn't .... a threat in your town.
12 When the interviewer posed a question about how best to .... the generation gap, her guest could make no feasible suggestions.

150

Test Two

B Words in use

Use the words and phrases on the left to complete the sentences on the right. Make sure the word or phrase is in the correct form. Some words are used more than once.

1 shoal / herd / swarm / pack

a I would hate to get in the way of a .... of stampeding cattle.
b Australian coral reefs are home to .... of brightly-coloured fish.
c .... of wolves can still be found roaming wild in Portugal.
d Being attacked by a .... of bees is no laughing matter.

2 slow / dim / fade / weaken

a As the pace .... it became obvious that the runner with the best sprint finish would win.
b Hopes of finding the divers alive were .... until they were spotted clinging to a rock.
c Please .... the lights before I turn on the projector.
d Despite the difficulties, their will to succeed has not ....

3 degree / rate / proportion / level / ratio

a The amount of work he did was out of all .... to what he was paid.
b If I were you, I'd take the complaint to the highest ....
c Given the high staff-patient .... at the hospital, your medical costs were quite reasonable.
d Do you know what the euro-yen exchange .... is?
e Not being able to answer Joan's question with any .... of certainty, I referred her to an authority on the subject.

4 shoulder / nose / finger / toe / skin / eye / hair / eyelid / hand

a Being such a snob, she turns her .... up at anyone without a public school education.
b Tom didn't bat a(n) .... when he was told he'd failed the course.
c Keep a(n) .... on the baby, please.
d Helena escaped a prison sentence by the .... of her teeth.
e Being lazy, Andrea needs teachers who will keep her constantly on her ....
f Cockroaches make my .... crawl.
g We'll keep our .... crossed for you when you go for the interview.
h Why was Paul given the cold .... by the rest of the class?
i They're pointing the .... at the marketing manager for the recent slump in sales.
j Harold came within a ....'s breadth of being selected for the national team.
k The match was expected to be difficult, but in the end we won .... down.

151

Test Two — Test your vocabulary

C Phrasal verbs
Match the phrasal verbs in bold with their definitions.

1. When I first met Jane, she **came across as** being rather shy. ....
2. Few people are qualified to **take up** a high profile job at NASA. ....
3. In order to remain camouflaged, a chameleon will **take on** the colour of its surroundings. ....
4. You need to **get round to** finishing your project as soon as possible. ....
5. The tidal wave **swept away** everything in its path when it hit the coast. ....
6. Make sure you **wrap up** well if you go out in this biting wind. ....
7. The exhibits will be **laid out** the week before this section of the museum reopens. ....
8. Unless he can **come up with** an explanation for the blood on his shirt, he will be the prime murder suspect. ....

a	arrange	e	find time to do
b	produce	f	destroy completely
c	begin to work at	g	make an impression
d	acquire	h	put on warmer clothes

D Preposition practice
Use the prepositions below to complete the sentences which follow. Some prepositions are used more than once.

in	of	on	to	with	out of	at

1. The course is aimed .... those wishing to get a firm grounding in computing.
2. Remaining faithful .... one's principles can be difficult when significant financial gains are involved.
3. You can't place too much emphasis .... the importance .... hard work.
4. The minister denied, ... no uncertain terms, that he had ever been associated .... anyone involved .... the scandal.
5. The book went .... print rather quickly due .... its disappointingly poor sales figures.
6. Unable to muster any resistance .... the temptation that lay before him, Jack ate the whole chocolate cake.

152

E Word building
Use the words in capitals at the end of each sentence to form a word that fits in the space in the same sentence.

1. Kelly felt .... embarrassed when she was forced to make a public apology to the editor. — DREAD
2. The .... population growth in Mexico city will lead to severe overcrowding. — EXPLODE
3. People with ginger hair .... turn red after sunbathing. — VARY
4. Only one .... of the burning building had to be treated in hospital. — OCCUPY
5. Engineers must be able to .... constructions even before they begin drawing up the plans for them. — VISUAL
6. New technology is rarely .... to anyone other than those who can afford it. — BENEFIT
7. Films like *Mullholland Drive* are largely .... because they are not logically sequenced. — COMPREHEND
8. It was a .... to discover how genetically similar humans and apes are. — REVEAL

F Tricky pairs
Compare each sentence by choosing the correct word.

1. Although the dolphin is *classed/considered* as a mammal, many people call it a fish.
2. For the main *dish/course*, I recommend sea bass.
3. The series *Friends* has been a *leading/smash* hit in several countries.
4. Pollution *inflicts/poses* a serious threat to our planet.
5. As soon as he *comes/goes* to his senses, he'll accept your generous offer.
6. Unaware of the *grave/lethal* danger they were in, the children made their way deeper into the forest.

Test Three

Test your vocabulary

Study the vocabulary used in **Practice Test 3** and then try the exercises below.

A   The right word

Complete each blank with the correct form of a word from the boxes. You may use a word more than once.

| vain | error | rage | tether | sense | insult | mind | dress |

1 Andy beat me at tennis and then, to add .... to injury, told me I should take up another sport.
2 When Mary went to live on a remote island, everyone thought she'd taken leave of her ....
3 One minute certain types of clothing are all the .... and the next they've gone out of fashion.
4 Mark must have been out of his .... to walk out of the exam after five minutes.
5 Carol flew into a .... when I accused her of cheating.
6 The bill was sent to me in ....
7 After trying in .... to persuade him to lend me his car, I was at the end of my ....
8 Our first performance is on Tuesday, so we're having the .... rehearsal the day before.

| acknowledge | call | shed | set | come | dawn | enrage | creak |

9   As soon as it .... on me that the boss's son .... the tune in the company, I kept away from him.
10 Terry had .... his heart on winning the tournament, but soon realised he had no chance.
11 Marion was .... by Colin's refusal to .... his mistake.
12 The floorboards on the old stage .... , which ruined the performance.
13 When the police eventually .... light on the murder investigation, the Wilsons had to .... to terms with the fact that their next-door neighbour was a killer.

| grossly | heavily | soaring | lost | clean |

14 Once you've been given a .... bill of health, you'll be discharged.
15 It was .... unfair of you to say that she was useless at her job.
16 He was .... dependent on his parents for money as he was too proud to get a job.
17 He realised it was a .... cause when he saw the strength of the competition.
18 .... inflation has dealt a serious blow to the economic stability of several South American countries.

Test Three

B Words in use

Use the words and phrases on the left to complete the sentences on the right. Make sure the word or phrase is in the correct form. Some words are used more than once.

1
- step
- pace
- rung
- stage

a He moved to another company to get his foot on the next .... of the ladder.
b Nowadays it is difficult to keep .... with all the technological innovations.
c At this .... in my career, I'd rather not take too many risks.
d I'd say their agreeing to cooperate is a .... in the right direction.
e The Kenyan set a blistering .... in the 5000 metres.

2
- attribute
- hail
- associate
- dedicate
- appoint
- assign

a Ecologists are .... to preserving fragile ecosystems.
b Almost everyone was astounded when Mr Johnson was .... headmaster.
c Nobody is absolutely sure who painted the portrait but I am sure it has been .... to Titian.
d The politician did not want to be .... with his brother's shady business deals.
e The project I have been .... will require a great deal of research.
f *Gone with the Wind* and *Casablanca* have been .... as classics by film critics.

3
- broadcast
- present
- feature
- characterise
- compose

a As far as I know, the match will be .... live.
b Having been .... in a TV documentary, she is often recognised in the street.
c Air is chiefly .... of oxygen and nitrogen.
d Being .... as a ham actor has not helped his career.
e Some meteorologists have .... the weather forecast on television with such enthusiasm that they have become celebrities.

4
- side
- fence
- wall
- hedge

a I'm not going to take .... in your argument, so leave me out of it.
b The grass is always greener on the other .... of the ....
c Stop sitting on the .... and make a decision.
d It pays to stay on her good ....
e We've been trying to make progress in the negotiations but we've apparently come up against a brick ....
f The garden, enclosed by a clipped ...., looks marvellous in spring.
g Disaster hasn't struck yet, but the writing is on the ....

155

Test Three — Test your vocabulary

C Phrasal verbs
Match the phrasal verbs in bold with their definitions.

1. Don't wait until prices **level off** before you buy gold. ....
2. Brian expects to be named company president when his father **steps down** next year. ....
3. The press **came in for** scathing criticism after publishing a sensitive government report. ....
4. Not being able to improve the animal's quality of life, the vet decided to **put** it **down**. ....
5. This junior tennis school **throws up** a great player now and again. ....
6. As soon as she **saw through** her fiancé's lies, she broke off their engagement. ....
7. I didn't **set out** to annoy Gill, but that's what I seem to have done. ....
8. Several new hotels **sprung up** after the new law was passed. ....
9. Don't **take on** any more work until you've recovered from your operation. ....
10. The twins **put away** most of their weekly allowance. ....

a	receive	f	intend at first
b	become stable	g	give up responsibility
c	produce	h	kill humanely
d	realise the truth about	i	save
e	assume responsibility for	j	appear suddenly

D Preposition practice
Use the prepositions below to complete the sentences which follow. Some prepositions are used more than once.

on	to	of	in	for	at

1. She always looks so depressed when she's dressed .... black.
2. May I have a word with you .... private, please?
3. Before you embark .... this venture, you must be totally committed to its success.
4. All the speakers were asked to restrict their speeches .... 15 minutes.
5. Only a lack .... determination can stop them from becoming world champions.
6. Nanotechnology is still .... its infancy.
7. While I was a guest at their house, their chauffeur was always .... my disposal.
8. I haven't decided which field of science to specialise .... yet.
9. Given the choice, I would always opt .... a skiing holiday.
10. Have you decided .... a name for your baby daughter?

156

E Word building

Use the words in capitals at the end of each sentence to form a word that fits in the space in the same sentence.

1	His broken nose only served to .... his rugged appearance.	ACCENT
2	Ken had never faced financial .... before, but his family rallied round to help him.	HARD
3	It was the .... he felt at the court's decision that brought about his lack of faith in the legal system.	JUST
4	A rabbit will .... refuse to move out of a beam of light if it is caught in one at night.	INSTINCT
5	Playing golf with an injured wrist will .... aggravate the problem.	DOUBT
6	As Gerald's profile is quite .... , two witnesses positively identified him as the perpetrator.	MISTAKE
7	Several stars are known to make .... contributions to worthy causes.	SUBSTANCE
8	Henry is now .... trying to apologise for his behaviour at Louise's wedding.	LATE

F Tricky pairs

Compare each sentence by choosing the correct word.

1 Too much exercise will do you more *damage/harm* than good.
2 Use a *fresh/pure* piece of paper for each question.
3 If the Prime Minister can convince the *general/ordinary* public he is sincere, he will be re-elected.
4 I *specifically/specially* told you to tidy up your room this morning.
5 There's no *telling/talking* what they'll do about the scandal but, whatever happens, it will remain a *telling/talking* point for some time to come.

Test Four

Test your vocabulary

Study the vocabulary used in **Practice Test 4** and then try the exercises below.

A The right word

Complete each blank with the correct form of a word from the boxes. You may use a word more than once.

| go | afflict | flood | take | pay | dice | fall |

1. You'll be .... with death if you swim in these shark-infested waters.
2. Unfortunately, the long-awaited match .... short of expectations.
3. Many tourists have .... prey to unscrupulous shopkeepers who overcharge them.
4. The climbers .... refuge in a cave during the storm.
5. Light .... in through the windows when we opened the shutters.
6. Nobody thought he'd still be at the top of the tennis rankings, but as the saying .... , you can't keep a good man down.
7. The school committee .... homage to their famous former pupil by naming the new gym after her.
8. Stroke victims are sometimes .... by an inability to speak clearly.

| touch | fish | nook | cat | kit | value | blend | course |

9. Always keep a tool .... in the boot of your car.
10. This will increase the market .... of your house.
11. With his unique .... of humour and management skills, he kept his employees happy.
12. The world-famous magician's act lent a .... of class to the show.
13. If Paul didn't tell anyone about the surprise party, then who let the .... out of the bag?
14. I felt like a .... out of water when I went to work in a foreign country.
15. We searched every .... and cranny for the lost earring.
16. We must decide on the right .... of action to take.

| long | squarely | perfectly | drastically | profound |

17. An embargo will have .... implications on the economy.
18. Harry's excuse seems .... plausible, so why don't you give him the benefit of the doubt?
19. It is far too easy to lay the blame .... on the shoulders of the management.
20. Fred is just the latest in a .... line of boyfriends Ann has humiliated.
21. Recent heavy snowfalls have .... affected transport networks.

Test Four

B Words in use

Use the words and phrases on the left to complete the sentences on the right. Make sure the word or phrase is in the correct form. Some words are used more than once.

1 unfamiliar
unknown
uncommon
unaccustomed

a I'm .... to walking to work, as I usually take the bus.
b He's .... with how we do things round here, so be patient with him.
c She's a very good artist, although she's relatively .... in this country.
d Burglaries are not .... in this part of the city.

2 summit
peak
crest
climax
heyday

a At the .... of their career, all their concerts were sell-outs.
b Mountain .... could clearly be seen in the distance.
c The surfer rode the .... of the wave until it broke on the shore.
d The Beatles were in their .... during the 1960s.
e As the situation reached a .... , serious decisions had to be made.
f A .... conference for all EU prime ministers is due to take place next week.
g The mountain climber was exhausted when he finally got to the ....

3 reduce
diminish
erode
deteriorate

a High winds and rough seas have .... the rocks along this shoreline.
b Relations between the two countries have .... in the past month.
c Little has been done to .... the volume of greenhouse gases in the atmosphere.
d Even after ten years as manager, his enthusiasm for the game has not ....

4 enrol
join
enlist
enter

a The competition organisers refuse to .... into any discussion of the results.
b There was no shortage of volunteers willing to .... in the army.
c The defendant .... a plea of 'not guilty' at the beginning of the trial.
d Why don't you .... a health and fitness club if you're out of shape.
e I haven't decided whether to .... on the archaeology course yet.

Test Four — Test your vocabulary

C Phrasal verbs

Match the phrasal verbs in bold with their definitions.

1. Only when her career **took off** did she buy a second home. ....
2. Whenever Duncan talks about politics, he gets **carried away** and starts shouting. ....
3. As the wind **got up**, we began to wonder whether it had been a wise decision to go sailing. ....
4. The best solution **put forward** was probably the simplest. ....
5. When cholera **broke out**, there was widespread panic. ....
6. Despite the hi-tech security system, someone managed to **break into** the building. ....
7. It was meant to be a secret, but Tony **gave it away** when he spoke to Rob last night. ....
8. Why did Trish **give up** playing tennis? ....
9. He **took on** more responsibilities than he could cope with. ....

a	propose	f	undertake, begin to have
b	appear suddenly	g	make known
c	forcibly enter	h	stop
d	begin to be successful	i	become stronger
e	lose control		

D Preposition practice

Use the prepositions below to complete the sentences which follow. Some prepositions are used more than once.

| in | of | by | from | on | to | for | with | at |

1. Everyone has to complete these forms, regardless .... nationality.
2. .... response to members' wishes, those responsible .... the fight have been banned .... the club.
3. We were .... no means the only ones to benefit .... the changes.
4. Mark was intent .... blaming everyone but himself .... the team's defeat.
5. This vast lake is home .... several species of fish.
6. As the meeting drew .... a close, the guest speaker reiterated his warning that fridges filled .... CFCs would have a great impact .... the environment.
7. .... the wake of recent developments, fresh vegetables will probably be .... a premium in the near future.
8. .... general terms, I'd say that the quality of food served at this restaurant is .... a par with that served in any other highly-recommended establishment.

E Word building

Use the words in capitals at the end of each sentence to form a word that fits in the space in the same sentence.

1 The .... use of genetically modified crops is playing havoc with other plants. — SPREAD
2 Ancient creatures like crocodiles are said to be at the end of their .... road. — EVOLVE
3 There are still thousands of marine creatures that have not been .... — CATEGORY
4 Alan's .... to help is indicative of his uncooperative nature. — WILL
5 As regards the living rooms in the flats I have seen, this one is .... large. — COMPARE
6 Your attitude left everyone .... ; it was totally uncalled for. — SPEAK
7 He is .... a kind person, although he can be a little abrupt sometimes. — ESSENCE
8 Honesty is something of a .... these days. — RARE

F Tricky pairs

Compare each sentence by choosing the correct word.

1 You'll do well to *steer/navigate* clear of that crowd.
2 Survival depends on the ability to *adopt/adapt* to the environment.
3 What *course/path* of action would you recommend?
4 Most of the students were well and *properly/truly* puzzled by the problem.
5 The compounds produced in this chemical *procedure/process* are well known.
6 Since I do not want to *alienate/expunge* myself from my colleagues, I am not prepared to blame anyone for this mess.

Test Five

Test your vocabulary

Study the vocabulary used in **Practice Test 5** and then try the exercises below.

A The right word
Complete each blank with the correct form of a word from the boxes. You may use a word more than once.

> leash   foothold   ravages   haven   exile   rank   quota

1 People who choose to live in a tax .... like Monaco are often called tax ....
2 He wanted to be one of the managers, not just one of the .... and file.
3 The entrepreneur was straining at the .... to get a .... in the new business.
4 When museum artefacts are not kept in proper conditions, they succumb to the .... of time.
5 Not getting your daily .... of vitamins may be harmful to your health.

> abundantly   confidential   relatively   thick   vast   painfully   silver   distant

6 The contents of this .... report have been leaked to the media.
7 Job offers came in .... and fast when people learnt that he had resigned from his job.
8 She's a .... cousin of mine on my mother's side.
9 The .... majority of the city's population live in apartment blocks.
10 She doesn't have to work because she was born with a .... spoon in her mouth.
11 If you consider the amount of work that goes into publishing educational books, they are .... cheap.
12 The process of searching the house was .... slow as they had to search every nook and cranny.
13 It's been made .... clear that I am expected to work harder.

> burst   shun   meet   give   keep

14 Many film stars pretend to .... publicity, but in reality they do anything to get it.
15 With ten people living here, our house is .... at the seams.
16 I tried not to laugh, but in the end I just couldn't .... a straight face.
17 Not paying enough attention to your diet may .... rise to health problems later on.
18 Nothing I do seems to .... with my parents' approval.

Test Five

B Words in use

Use the words and phrases on the left to complete the sentences on the right. Make sure the word or phrase is in the correct form.

1
- inheritance
- legacy
- heirloom
- keepsake

a Henrietta's .... amounted to over £2 million.
b This diamond brooch is a family .... ; it once belonged to my great great grandmother.
c A whole generation of children with stunted growth is the .... of the civil war.
d My locket is a .... given to me by an old friend.

2
- essential
- vital
- significant
- fundamental

a Since no .... organs were damaged in the crash, a full recovery is expected.
b Several .... archaeological finds have been made in the Gobi Desert.
c It is .... that you contact him before 2pm today.
d Every child has a .... need for a secure home environment.

3
- cutting
- piercing
- throbbing
- splitting

a As we entered the deserted mansion, a .... scream shattered the silence.
b Jack's .... comments made him more enemies than friends.
c My .... fingers were the result of trapping my hand in the car door.
d A .... headache made it impossible for me to concentrate on my work.

4
- subjected
- engaged
- engrossed
- marvelled
- exposed

a Terry was so .... in his book that he didn't hear me come in.
b The audience .... at the ballerina's grace.
c We were .... to unacceptable treatment while on holiday last year.
d Once you have been .... to corruption it can become a way of life.
e Mark and Jenny were .... in conversation in the library.

Test Five — Test your vocabulary

C Phrasal verbs
Match the phrasal verbs in bold with their definitions.

1. When winter **sets in**, travelling in some northern countries becomes extremely difficult. ....
2. **Delving into** our ancestors' behaviour can reveal some unpleasant facts. ....
3. As news of the hijack **filtered through**, people began phoning the airline for more details. ....
4. A survey has to be carefully planned before it is **carried out**. ....
5. They won't be able to **get by** on a reduced pension. ....
6. Whoever **drew up** these plans failed to take into account the current economic climate. ....
7. We must **get round** to painting the cellar. ....
8. The possibility that the burglary was an inside job has not yet been **ruled out**. ....
9. Some authors manage to **churn out** work effortlessly. ....

a	research thoroughly	f	arrive slowly
b	conduct	g	prepare
c	exclude	h	find time to do
d	become established	i	produce in large quantities
e	manage		

D Preposition practice
Use the prepositions below to complete the sentences which follow. Some prepositions are used more than once.

to	with	on	into	across	in	at	against

1. The children were reduced .... tears when their teacher flew .... a rage and decided to vent her anger .... them.
2. This research should shed some light .... the reasons for the increase .... crime in this area.
3. Animals in captivity should be allowed to feed .... prey similar .... those they would find in the wild.
4. It seems plain .... me that if she has to hold the book .... arm's length to read it, she has a problem with her eyesight.
5. It was a race .... time for the presidential candidate to get his message .... to undecided voters.
6. .... some extent, it can be a disadvantage for police to confront a suspect .... incriminating evidence early in an investigation.

164

E Word building
Use the words in capitals at the end of each sentence to form a word that fits in the space in the same sentence.

1 Working .... on the project for several weeks, we achieved a great deal.　　METHOD
2 What are the .... of the proposed economic package?　　IMPLY
3 Despite being .... three to one by a rival gang, they showed no fear.　　NUMBER
4 I found some of the ingredients used in local dishes quite ....　　REPEL
5 Transfer of .... can take up to a month.　　OWN
6 Reporting news without the utmost care can result in ....　　CONCEIVE
7 It was George's .... to concentrate for any length of time that cost him the exam.　　ABLE
8 Carol is .... when she's in a bad mood.　　APPROACH

F Tricky pairs
Compare each sentence by choosing the correct word.

1 Many people have almost *choked/drowned* in bath water.
2 You can leave as soon as the other security guard comes to *relinquish/relieve* you.
3 The professor *hit/knocked* the nail on the head when he said thinking was an art.
4 There were people from all *walks/paths* of life at the conference.
5 If he can't take a *clue/hint*, then I'll just have to be blunt and tell him to leave.
6 These walls could do with a *brush/lick* of paint.

Test Six — Test your vocabulary

Study the vocabulary used in **Practice Test 6** and then try the exercises below.

A The right word

Complete each blank with the correct form of a word from the boxes. You may use a word more than once.

| take | pass | desire | wage | spark | spill | come | give | release |

1 You had better .... clean about the missing software or we'll all be in trouble.
2 Although current events may .... a crisis in the region, the government appears to be unconcerned.
3 The safety measures that have so far been .... at the factory leave much to be ...., so unless new laws are ...., high levels of pollution will continue to cause health problems.
4 Don't forget to .... your handbrake before moving off and make sure you .... way to traffic on the main road.
5 Sniffer dogs will play a key role in the war of attrition to be .... on smugglers.
6 By .... the beans, Margot lost many of her friends who felt she'd betrayed them.

| harsh | deeply | small | short | slight | high | utterly |

7 Graham believes he is held in .... esteem, but the .... reality is that his colleagues are now .... disgusted with his recent inappropriate behaviour.
8 Despite being .... moved by pictures of starving children, she never gave any money to charity.
9 Not having to worry about money, they spent a .... fortune on caviar.
10 Water is in .... supply in many parts of Africa.
11 He has a .... limp as a result of a sporting accident when he was younger.

| truck | skin | brunt | teeth | eye | anger |

12 Sheila would have no .... with those colleagues she believed to be ineffective.
13 It's best to stay away when Alan throws one of his temper tantrums because he'll only vent his .... on you and you'll have to bear the .... of his criticism.
14 Jane managed to catch the last train by the .... of her teeth.
15 Whether it is acceptable to lie through your .... when you're in the public .... is a matter for discussion.
16 We were soaked to the .... when we were caught in a heavy downpour.

Test Six

B Words in use

Use the words and phrases on the left to complete the sentences on the right. Make sure the word or phrase is in the correct form. Some words are used more than once.

1 shed / cast / spread / inflict

a What kind of person enjoys .... pain on others?
b It is hoped that new evidence will .... light on the incident.
c Butter is more difficult to .... than margarine.
d Who was responsible for .... these rumours in the office?
e The results of the trials .... doubt on the effectiveness of the method.

2 span / spell / period / time / shift

a You'll be told about the decision all in good ....
b I hate working the night .... , especially in winter.
c Last year's extended cold .... meant higher fuel bills.
d Having a short attention .... , young children cannot concentrate on one activity for very long.
e The injured animal had to undergo a short adjustment .... before being released into the wild.

3 harvest / gather / reap / plough / yield

a You can have my old computer as it's only .... dust in my attic.
b The poor do not always .... the benefits of aid sent to developing countries.
c Extra employees are taken on when the crops are ....
d These fields .... sufficient rice for all the farmer's needs.
e Don't expect to .... the rewards of your hard work immediately.
f .... the field was difficult because it was stony.

4 shrug / hunch / hug / stoop / huddle

a We .... together to keep warm in the biting wind.
b Seeing a £5 note on the floor, I .... to pick it up.
c When asked the reason for his actions, the prisoner just .... his shoulders and smiled.
d Catherine always .... her friends when she hasn't seen them for a while.
e Frank .... his shoulders as he stood waiting for a bus in a snowstorm.

167

Test Six

Test your vocabulary

C Phrasal verbs

Match the phrasal verbs in bold with their definitions.

1 What the eye witness said **tied in with** the arresting officer's report. ....
2 If you don't **brush up on** your Spanish, your trip to Argentina will be all the more difficult. ....
3 Being vain, the film star **lapped up** all the media attention. ....
4 Terry **stood up to** his boss and was never humiliated by her again. ....
5 I must have **dozed off** because I didn't see the end of the film. ....
6 The old cinema has been **turned into** a supermarket. ....
7 As I am so busy, I find it almost impossible to **set aside** time for leisure activities. ....
8 It's freezing outside so **wrap up** before you go out. ....
9 The researchers do not expect to **come up against** any more obstacles. ....
10 Whole populations of several species have been **wiped out** after their habitats have been invaded. ....

a	fall asleep	f	destroy completely
b	improve	g	be in agreement with
c	spare	h	enjoy greatly
d	resist	i	encounter
e	put on warm clothes	j	convert

D Preposition practice

Use the prepositions below to complete the sentences which follow. Some prepositions are used more than once.

| for | to | in | of | at | with | against | on | from |

1 This new medicine should provide relief .... those who suffer .... arthritis and are .... pain most of the time.
2 Experts cannot reach agreement .... whether the painting should be attributed .... Gauguin or not.
3 Brenda will protest .... any company that is associated .... experimenting on animals.
4 Sally's not just capable .... causing trouble, she's adept .... it.
5 Denying locals access .... the coast will deprive them .... their livelihood.
6 Showing a blatant disregard .... the highway code is not only hazardous .... other road users but to the driver .... question as well.
7 .... first glance, I thought the picture quality on your television was inferior .... that on mine, but now I have a distinct preference .... the make you have.

Test Six

E Word building

Use the words in capitals at the end of each sentence to form a word that fits in the space in the same sentence.

1 I find having to wait for people who are always late quite .... TOLERATE

2 Jane has worked .... to protect chimps. TIRE

3 Your .... behaviour has not gone unnoticed. EXAMPLE

4 The .... of the unpopular tax was welcomed by the majority of the population. ABOLISH

5 Jerry has been .... to act on his parents' behalf in legal matters. POWER

6 Finding the new regime's attitude to foreigners most .... , she decided to leave. TASTE

7 During her lifetime, Mother Theresa .... virtues that few people have. BODY

8 The .... of some animals in captivity is a sign that the captors are uncivilised. TREAT

F Tricky pairs

Compare each sentence by choosing the correct word.

1 Take a look at the price *label/tag* before you decide to buy it.

2 In the normal *path/course* of events, the parade should go smoothly.

3 The situation will only be *exaggerated/exacerbated* if you protest.

4 Harold's reluctance to cooperate was a *sign/gesture* of things to come.

5 Many people have to *supplement/subsidise* their income with an evening job.

6 Ray began his professional football career with a club in the second *category/division*.

7 Several witnesses have been arrested for attempting to pervert the *course/way* of justice.

169

Test One

Photographs for the Speaking Paper

170

Photographs for the Speaking Paper

Test Two

171

Test Three

Photographs for the Speaking Paper

172

Photographs for the Speaking Paper

Test Four

173

Test Five

Photographs for the Speaking Paper

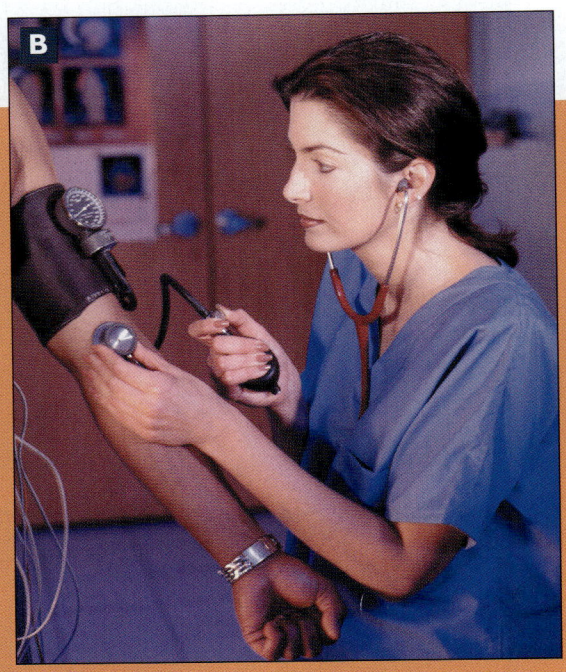

174

Photographs for the Speaking Paper

Test Six

175

First published by New Editions 2003 - 0605

New Editions
37 Bagley Wood Road
Kennington
Oxford
England

New Editions
PO Box 76101
17110 Nea Smyrni
Athens
Greece

Tel: (+30) 210 9883156
Fax: (+30) 210 9880223
E-mail: enquiries@new-editions.com
Website: www.new-editions.com

Text, design and illustrations © New Editions 2003

Published under licence from Howsbury Enterprises Private Limited

ISBN Student's Book   960-403-110-4
ISBN Teacher's Book   960-403-112-0

All rights reserved. No part of this publication may be reproduced, stored in a retrieval system, or transmitted in any form or by any means, electronic, mechanical, photocopying, recording, or otherwise, without the prior written permission of the publishers. Any person who carries out any unauthorised act in relation to this publication may be liable to criminal prosecution and civil claims for damages.

We are grateful to the following for permission to reproduce copyright material:

Desmond Morris for an extract from his book 'Manwatching'.

New International Newspapers Ltd for extracts from the articles 'Come on, boys, at the treble' by S. Llewellyn © The Times, 14.12.2002, 'From train set to training' by Tony Cascarino © The Times, 23.12.2002.

New Scientist for extracts from the articles 'Love on a wire' by P. Collins, December 2002, 'Soundless music' by Nick Hamer, December 2002, Electric paper by Jonathan Fildes, January 2003.

BBC History Magazine for 'James VI' by Alan Stewart, March 2003. This article appears in the March 2003 issue of BBC History Magazine. For subscriptions and back issues +44 (0) 1795 414 728.

The Observer Newpaper for extracts from the articles 'Beauty in the land of the polar bear picnic' by Jamie Doward, 'Wanna be in our gang?' by Robert McCrum, 'Monaco's millionaire mile' by Paul Webster, 24.11.2002, 'Lost for words' by Robin McKie, 12.1.2003, 'My little tip for greedy hotels' by Joanne O' Connor, 2.3.2003.

Natural History Magazine for extracts from the articles 'Requiem for a heavyweight' by Juan Luis Arsuaga, 'The unselfish genome', January 2003.

The Ecologist for an extract from the article 'Appetite for destruction' by Dr Mike Shanahan, 22.3.2003.

Every effort has been made to trace copyright holders. If any have been inadvertently overlooked, the publishers will be pleased to make the necessary acknowledgements at the first opportunity.

NEW CAMBRIDGE PROFICIENCY PRACTICE TESTS 2 ANSWER KEY

by Nicholas Stephens and Rachel Finnie

TEST 1

READING

Part 1
1 A; 2 B; 3 D; 4 C; 5 B; 6 D; 7 B; 8 D; 9 A; 10 D; 11 B; 12 C; 13 B; 14 A; 15 B; 16 D; 17 C; 18 A

Part 2
19 D; 20 C; 21 C; 22 A; 23 B; 24 A; 25 B; 26 A

Part 3
27 D; 28 F; 29 A; 30 H; 31 E; 32 G; 33 C

Part 4
34 C; 35 D; 36 B; 37 D; 38 A; 39 B; 40 B

USE OF ENGLISH

Part 1
1 ON/DURING; 2 BLOW; 3 ITS; 4 FULL; 5 SO/AS; 6 TIMES; 7 ANOTHER; 8 ALL; 9 ON; 10 TO; 11 SUFFERING; 12 ALTHOUGH/WHILE; 13 LITTLE; 14 WENT; 15 COST

Part 2
16 SIMPLICITY; 17 ENSURE; 18 ELUSIVE; 19 ALLIANCE; 20 UNINSPIRING; 21 ENTITLED; 22 INSIGHT; 23 NUMEROUS/INNUMERABLE; 24 RELENTLESSLY; 25 INDISPENSABLE

Part 3
26 SHORT; 27 BREAK; 28 PRESENT; 29 ODD; 30 BEAR; 31 WITHDRAW

Part 4
32 to shed light on what; 33 would rather you didn't bring; 34 be considered valid unless the president's signature; 35 has resulted in the closure of; 36 are incapable of discussing money without shouting; 37 turn over a new leaf and not; 38 is never at a loss for; 39 goes without saying that Serena will make

Part 5
40 that they are still experimenting; 41 they must retain their traditional image as well as explore the benefits of genetic engineering; 42 It was given two genes from a bacterium/Escherichia coli; 43 to show that the gentic modification has been successful; 44 The summary should include the following points using the student's own words:
- change the taste and quality of the product
- protect plants against disease
- allow plants to grow in hostile environments
- improve crop yields

LISTENING

Part 1
1 B; 2 C; 3 B; 4 C; 5 A; 6 C; 7 A; 8 B

Part 2
9 living; 10 retail; 11 pay more; 12 small business; 13 prices; 14 hygenic; 15 hidden; 16 inequalities; 17 Growers

Part 3
18 B; 19 A; 20 C; 21 C; 22 A

Part 4
23 B; 24 M; 25 B; 26 M; 27 B; 28 N

TEST 2

READING

Part 1
1 A; 2 C; 3 B; 4 A; 5 C; 6 C; 7 B; 8 D; 9 A; 10 A; 11 D; 12 A; 13 C; 14 A; 15 D; 16 B; 17 B; 18 A

Part 2
19 A; 20 C; 21 D; 22 B; 23 B; 24 D; 25 D; 26 B

Part 3
27 F; 28 H; 29 C; 30 B; 31 D; 32 A; 33 G

Part 4
34 A; 35 D; 36 B; 37 B; 38 A; 39 C; 40 C

USE OF ENGLISH

Part 1
1 LIKE; 2 THOSE; 3 OVER/ACROSS/THROUGHOUT; 4 MAKES; 5 HOWEVER; 6 SAME; 7 DUE/DOWN; 8 NOTHING/LITTLE; 9 WAY; 10 EYELID; 11 AWAY; 12 FAVOUR; 13 HAND; 14 TO; 15 EVER

Part 2
16 SYNONYMOUS; 17 SADDENED; 18 UNAPPRECIATED; 19 RESPONSE; 20 INCOMPREHENSIBLE; 21 EXPLANATORY; 22 VISUALISING; 23 INSTINCTIVELY; 24 REVELATION; 25 ACCESSIBLE

Part 3
26 COUNT; 27 STAND; 28 SPOT; 29 CHARGE; 30 LIGHT; 31 AUTHORITY

Part 4
32 got round to replying; 33 gave John the impression you would hand in; 34 fail to understand/see how we will benefit from; 35 the season has finished will the manager; 36 can fend for themselves despite/in spite of; 37 was given the cold shoulder by; 38 have known better than to lend; 39 can't/cannot tell the difference between

Part 5
40 droves, cornucopia; 41 conservation orders could be relaxed or withdrawn; 42 New prosperity has brought with it the need for new buildings as well as the downside of increased tourism.; They are unwanted/have no place in that area.; 44 The summary should include the following points using the student's own words:
- plot may be unsuitable due to terrain or conservation orders
- plot may not have a building on it
- plot may not be accompanied by correct permits
- views may be spoilt by new building and cruise liners

LISTENING

Part 1
1 B; 2 B; 3 B; 4 A; 5 A; 6 B; 7 C; 8 A

Part 2
9 sky; 10 27; 11 twice; 12 at least four; 13 LCD/Liquid Crystal Display; 14 your path; 15 estimated time; 16 computer (system); 17 being abducted

Part 3
18 A; 19 B; 20 C; 21 C; 22 D

Part 4
23 B; 24 J; 25 B; 26 F; 27 J; 28 J

TEST 3

READING

Part 1
1 A; 2 C; 3 B; 4 C; 5 B; 6 C; 7 C; 8 D; 9 B; 10 A; 11 B; 12 D; 13 B; 14 A; 15 D; 16 C; 17 B; 18 C

Part 2
19 C; 20 C; 21 B; 22 A; 23 B; 24 B; 25 C; 26 D

Part 3
27 G; 28 H; 29 E; 30 C; 31 B; 32 F; 33 D

Part 4
34 A; 35 C; 36 A; 37 C; 38 C; 39 A; 40 B

USE OF ENGLISH

Part 1
1 OTHERS; 2 LIKE; 3 CHOOSE; 4 FOR; 5 END; 6 TAKE; 7 WERE; 8 AFTER; 9 ONLY; 10 COULD; 11 WHICH; 12 TO; 13 SET; 14 LIKELY; 15 OWN

Part 2
16 IMPRISONMENT; 17 HARDSHIP; 18 DEPRIVATION; 19 INJUSTICE; 20 SCHOOLING; 21 PARLIAMENTARY; 22 INSTINCTIVELY; 23 READINGS; 24 SUBSTANTIAL; 25 UNDOUBTEDLY

Part 3
26 GATHER; 27 OVERLOOK; 28 PROVE; 29 WIDE; 30 VOLUME; 31 MATTER

Part 4
32 planning, the venture will not get off; 33 have not been on speaking terms; 34 into a rage when she found/on finding; 35 transfer is subject to his/him; 36 did not see through her daughter's; 37 was absolute silence when/after the manager told/informed; 38 bears little/no resemblance to; 39 never accuse you of telling

Part 5
40 legendary, headline-grabber; 41 the fact that size is not everything; 42 innocuous-looking, benign, appealing; 43 stay out of fights; 44 The summary should include the following points using the student's own words:
- both use poison that aids digestion
- cone snail hides and waits for prey
- it paralyses prey and eats it immediately
- taipan goes after prey and then releases it
- it follows scent of poison to find it later

LISTENING

Part 1
1 A; 2 C; 3 C; 4 B; 5 A; 6 B; 7 B; 8 A

Part 2
9 particle physics; 10 sheets; 11 curtains; 12 flames; 13 weather; 14 electrical discharges; 15 cold(er); 16 little ice age; 17 concept

Part 3
18 B; 19 A; 20 C; 21 C; 22 A

Part 4
23 F; 24 E; 25 F; 26 E; 27 B; 28 E

TEST 4

READING

Part 1
1 A; 2 A; 3 D; 4 B; 5 D; 6 C; 7 B; 8 D; 9 A; 10 A; 11 C; 12 B; 13 B; 14 A; 15 D; 16 A; 17 C; 18 B

Part 2
19 C; 20 A; 21 A; 22 C; 23 A; 24 A; 25 C; 26 B

Part 3
27 A; 28 B; 29 F; 30 H; 31 C; 32 G; 33 E

Part 4
34 C; 35 D; 36 B; 37 C; 38 A; 39 C; 40 D

USE OF ENGLISH

Part 1
1 SIDE; 2 AS; 3 KINDS/SORTS; 4 RELIED/DEPENDED; 5 WHEREVER; 6 GOES; 7 SO; 8 TO; 9 EVEN; 10 IN; 11 BEING; 12 UNTIL; 13 OUT; 14 WHICH; 15 COUNTRY(SIDE)

Part 2
16 UNFOUNDED; 17 WIDESPREAD; 18 CHILDHOOD; 19 COMPARATIVELY; 20 PASSING; 21 GUIDANCE; 22 CATEGORISED; 23 DISORDERS; 24 UNWILLINGNESS; 25 HANDFUL

Part 3
26 RING; 27 ANSWERED; 28 BOARD; 29 JUMP; 30 SPREAD; 31 FAIR

Part 4
32 could not come to terms with the; 33 has been a definite improvement in Maria's pronunciation; 34 must remain in control of the situation at; 35 were all taken aback by the speed; 36 firm belief (that) Veronica had no knowledge of; 37 have gone through the roof; 38 puts his success down to a/his good; 39 to refrain from smoking

Part 5
40 stress affects different people in different ways; 41 by realising that it exists/is there; 42 encourage us to achieve more; 43 'what they advise is not equally applicable to every person'; 44 The summary should include the following points using the student's own words: what causes it
- our reactions to events in our lives, either physical or emotional
- changes in our personal lives
- situations around us involving time, money, noise, etc
how to alleviate it
- first, be aware that one has a problem with stress
- change or reduce the things that cause one stress
- try to react differently to things that cause one stress
- try to keep healthy in order to be able to be resilient to stressful situations and cope with problems

LISTENING

Part 1
1 A; 2 C; 3 B; 4 B; 5 B; 6 C; 7 B; 8 A

Part 2
9 a million; 10 amount/quantity; 11 groups/group raids; 12 underground channels; 13 sweep; 14 sting; 15 a ball; 16 (the) ants (themselves); 17 insects

Part 3
18 B; 19 C; 20 A; 21 C; 22 B

Part 4
23 A; 24 B; 25 B; 26 A; 27 B; 28 A

TEST 5

READING

Part 1
1 C; 2 A; 3 A; 4 C; 5 B; 6 D; 7 A; 8 D; 9 D; 10 B; 11 C; 12 C; 13 D; 14 C; 15 B; 16 B; 17 A; 18 B

Part 2
19 D; 20 A; 21 D; 22 D; 23 B; 24 B; 25 A; 26 B

Part 3
27 E; 28 G; 29 C; 30 F; 31 A; 32 B; 33 D

Part 4
34 C; 35 B; 36 D; 37 A; 38 D; 39 C; 40 D

USE OF ENGLISH

Part 1
1 FINDING; 2 GET; 3 CARRIED; 4 OVER/ABOUT/ APPROXIMATELY; 5 HAS; 6 EACH; 7 VERY; 8 TO; 9 ON; 10 GIVEN; 11 UP; 12 AGED; 13 RATHER; 14 AWAY; 15 WHOSE

Part 2
16 PORTRAYAL; 17 AUTHENTICITY; 18 MISCONCEPTIONS; 19 DISTORTION(S); 20 REPULSIVE; 21 UNHYGIENIC; 22 DIVERSION; 23 METHODICALLY; 24 EYESIGHT; 25 INABILITY

Part 3
26 FALLS; 27 THING; 28 GREAT; 29 PLAIN; 30 ACCEPTED; 31 FLEW

Part 4
32 will get/be given the green light; 33 failure has been ruled out (by the experts); 34 expressed his annoyance at being left; 35 planned the venture properly, you would have made; 36 (in) keeping a straight face; 37 effectively, she always gets/can always get her message; 38 the nail on the head when he; 39 in the dark about the merger except

Part 5
40 to show the widespread application of Six Hat thinking; 41 it diminishes the importance of ego and pride; 42 (without perception, intelligence) is useless; 43 fuzzy, barrier; 44 The summary should include the following points using the student's own words:
- trying to think in several directions at once
- ego and pride
- using logic too widely
- lack of perception
- preconceived ideas/not listening to others

LISTENING

Part 1
1 B; 2 A; 3 A; 4 B; 5 B; 6 B; 7 C; 8 A

Part 2
9 Indian Ocean; 10 fragile; 11 over-exploitation; 12 climatic change; 13 ten minutes; 14 volcanic land; 15 plants, trees; 16 sea level; 17 respect

Part 3
18 B; 19 C; 20 A; 21 B; 22 A

Part 4
23 B; 24 F; 25 T; 26 B; 27 B; 28 F

TEST 6

READING

Part 1
1 C; 2 D; 3 A; 4 B; 5 D; 6 C; 7 D; 8 C; 9 D; 10 A; 11 C; 12 B; 13 B; 14 B; 15 D; 16 C; 17 A; 18 C

Part 2
19 D; 20 B; 21 C; 22 D; 23 A; 24 B; 25 A; 26 D

Part 3
27 B; 28 E; 29 A; 30 C; 31 F; 32 D; 33 G

Part 4
34 A; 35 A; 36 C; 37 A; 38 D; 39 B; 40 B

USE OF ENGLISH

Part 1
1 ONE; 2 MATTER; 3 TAKEN; 4 IN; 5 LESS; 6 FAR; 7 WHOSE; 8 HIGHEST; 9 AGAINST; 10 RATHER; 11 MAKING; 12 POSSIBLE; 13 UNLIKE; 14 TO; 15 POINT

Part 2
16 FAILURE; 17 LEGENDARY; 18 DISASTEROUSLY; 19 DISAPPOINTINGLY; 20 BEHAVIOUR; 21 EXEMPLARY; 22 EMBODIED; 23 MIS/MALTREATMENT; 24 TIRELESSLY; 25 ABOLITION

Part 3
26 HIGH; 27 RELEASE; 28 COLLAPSED; 29 HIT; 30 LED; 31 WAY

Part 4
32 treatment led to a dramatic improvement in; 33 she saw the body did it dawn on; 34 the skin of her teeth that she succeeded; 35 to come up against financial problems, would; 36 bore the brunt of the criticism; 37 hinged on their/them being able to raise; 38 was not prepared to go into; 39 last term that she made an attempt

Part 5
40 it is becoming accepted/it is no longer mocked; 41 to show that it is not needed any longer (like a worker who is surplus to requirements); 42 messages arrive unexpectedly; 43 'the brain waves of the recipient change to match those of the sender'; 44 The summary should include the following points using the student's own words:
- training the mind
- members of the same family, particularly twins
- an inability to communicate in normal ways
- in times of trouble
- in a dream state

LISTENING

Part 1
1 B; 2 C; 3 A; 4 B; 5 B; 6 A; 7 B; 8 B

Part 2
9 crime scenes; 10 distinguishing; 11 (relative) hardness; 12 crush; 13 (even) (more) clues; 14 unique; 15 the sequence; 16 three-dimensional; 17 make, model

Part 3
18 D; 19 C; 20 A; 21 C; 22 B

Part 4
23 J; 24 M; 25 B; 26 J; 27 B; 28 J

TEST YOUR VOCABULARY

Test 1

A
1 bandwagon; 2 risk; 3 wind; 4 leaf; 5 fear; 6 hold; 7 reaping; 8 goes; 9 shed, came; 10 gather; 11 capture; 12 run; 13 tidy, short; 14 short; 15 wide; 16 odd; 17 full; 18 remotely; 19 positively; 20 fully; 21 simply

B
1 a In terms of; b by means of; c in line with; d In keeping with; 2 a remotely; b virtually; c roughly; d barely; 3 a whole; b total; c full; d complete; 4 a average; b lead; c prime; d top; 5 a stand; b battle; c conflict; d fight

C
1 i; 2 a; 3 g; 4 j; 5 b; 6 f; 7 e; 8 c; 9 h; 10 d

D
1 out of; 2 on; 3 to; 4 by; 5 from; 6 in; 7 in; 8 towards; 9 in; 10 to

E
1 simplicity; 2 irresistible; 3 alliance; 4 respiratory;
5 demoralising; 6 insight; 7 ensure; 8 indispensable

F
1 rates; 2 foregone; 3 highly; 4 fear; 5 surpassed; 6 dominant

Test 2

A
1 prior; 2 previous; 3 beforehand; 4 advance; 5 fierce; 6 deadly;
7 thorny; 8 rival; 9 gave, fend; 10 stand; 11 count, pose; 12 bridge

B
1 a herd; b shoal; c Packs; d swarm; 2 a slowed; b fading;
c dim; d weakened; 3 a proportion; b level; c ratio; d rate;
e degree; 4 a nose; b eyelid; c eye; d skin; e toes; f skin;
g fingers; h shoulder; i finger; j hair; k hands

C
1 g; 2 c; 3 d; 4 e; 5 f; 6 h; 7 a; 8 b

D
1 at; 2 to; 3 on, of; 4 in, with, in; 5 out of, to; 6 to

E
1 dreadfully; 2 explosive; 3 invariably; 4 occupant; 5 visualise;
6 beneficial; 7 incomprehensible; 8 revelation

F
1 classed; 2 course; 3 smash; 4 poses; 5 comes; 6 grave

Test 3

A
1 insult; 2 senses; 3 rage; 4 mind; 5 rage; 6 error; 7 vain, tether;
8 dress; 9 dawned, called; 10 set; 11 enraged, acknowledge;
12 creaked; 13 shed, come; 14 clean; 15 grossly; 16 heavily;
17 lost; 18 Soaring

B
1 a rung; b pace; c stage; d step; e pace; 2 a dedicated;
b appointed; c attributed; d associated; e assigned; f hailed; 3 a broadcast; b featured; c composed; d characterised; e presented;
4 a sides; b side, fence; c fence; d side; e wall; f hedge; g wall

C
1 b; 2 g; 3 a; 4 h; 5 c; 6 d; 7 f; 8 j; 9 e; 10 i

D
1 in; 2 in; 3 on; 4 to; 5 of; 6 in; 7 at; 8 in; 9 for; 10 on

E
1 accentuate; 2 hardship; 3 injustice; 4 instinctively;
5 undoubtedly; 6 unmistakable; 7 substantial; 8 belatedly

F
1 harm; 2 fresh; 3 general; 4 specifically; 5 telling, talking

Test 4

A
1 dicing; 2 fell; 3 fallen; 4 took; 5 flooded; 6 goes; 7 paid;
8 afflicted; 9 kit; 10 value; 11 blend; 12 touch; 13 cat; 14 fish;
15 nook; 16 course; 17 profound; 18 perfectly; 19 squarely;
20 long; 21 drastically

B
1 a unaccustomed; b unfamiliar; c unknown; d uncommon; 2 a peak; b peaks; c crest; d heyday; e climax; f summit; g summit

3 a eroded; b deteriorated; c reduce; d diminished; 4 a enter;
b enlist; c entered; d join; e enrol

C
1 d; 2 e; 3 i; 4 a; 5 b; 6 c; 7 g; 8 h; 9 f

D
1 of; 2 In, for, from; 3 by, from; 4 on, for; 5 to; 6 to, with, on;
7 In, at; 8 In, on

E
1 widespread; 2 evolutionary; 3 categorised; 4 unwillingness;
5 comparatively; 6 speechless; 7 essentially; 8 rarity

F
1 steer; 2 adapt; 3 course; 4 truly; 5 process; 6 alienate

Test 5

A
1 haven, exiles; 2 rank; 3 foothold; 4 ravages; 5 quota;
6 confidential; 7 thick; 8 distant; 9 vast; 10 silver; 11 relatively;
12 painfullt; 13 abundantly; 14 shun; 15 bursting; 16 keep;
17 give; 18 meet

B
1 a inheritance; b heirloom; c legacy; d keepsake; 2 a vital;
b significant; c essential/vital; d fundamental; 3 a piercing;
b cutting; c throbbing; d splitting; 4 a engrossed; b marvelled;
c subjected; d exposed; e engaged

C
1 d; 2 a; 3 f; 4 b; 5 e; 6 g; 7 h; 8 c; 9 i

D
1 to, into, on; 2 on, in; 3 on, to; 4 to, at; 5 against, across;
6 To, with

E
1 methodically; 2 implications; 3 outnumbered; 4 repulsive;
5 ownership; 6 misconceptions; 7 inability; 8 unapproachable

F
1 drowned; 2 relieve; 3 hit; 4 walks; 5 hint; 6 lick

Test 6

A
1 come; 2 spark; 3 taken, desired, passed; 4 release; 5 waged;
6 spilling; 7 high, harsh, utterly; 8 deeply; 9 small; 10 short;
11 slight; 12 truck; 13 anger, brunt; 14 skin; 15 teeth, eye; 16 skin

B
1 a inflicting; b shed; c spread; d spreading; e cast; 2 a time;
b shift; c spell d span; e period; 3 a gathering; b reap;
c harvested; d yield; e reap; f Ploughing; 4 a huddled; b stooped; c shrugged; d hugs; e hunched

C
1 g; 2 b; 3 h; 4 d; 5 a; 6 j; 7 c; 8 e; 9 i; 10 f

D
1 for, from, in; 2 on, to; 3 against, with; 4 of, at; 5 to, of;
6 for, to, in; 7 At, to, for

E
1 intolerable; 2 tirelessly; 3 exemplary; 4 abolition;
5 empowered; 6 distasteful; 7 embodied; 8 mis/maltreatment

F
1 tag; 2 course; 3 exacerbated; 4 sign; 5 supplement; 6 division;
7 course